Advanced Introduction to Cybersecurity Law

Elgar Advanced Introductions are stimulating and thoughtful introductions to major fields in the social sciences, business and law, expertly written by the world's leading scholars. Designed to be accessible yet rigorous, they offer concise and lucid surveys of the substantive and policy issues associated with discrete subject areas.

The aims of the series are two-fold: to pinpoint essential principles of a particular field, and to offer insights that stimulate critical thinking. By distilling the vast and often technical corpus of information on the subject into a concise and meaningful form, the books serve as accessible introductions for undergraduate and graduate students coming to the subject for the first time. Importantly, they also develop well-informed, nuanced critiques of the field that will challenge and extend the understanding of advanced students, scholars and policy-makers.

For a full list of titles in the series please see the back of the book. Recent titles in the series include:

U.S. Environmental Law
E. Donald Elliott and Daniel C. Esty

Gentrification
Chris Hamnett

Family Policy
Chiara Saraceno

Law and Psychology
Tom R. Tyler

Advertising
Patrick De Pelsmacker

New Institutional Economics
Claude Ménard and Mary M. Shirley

The Sociology of Sport
Eric Anderson and Rory Magrath

The Sociology of Peace Processes
John D. Brewer

Social Protection
James Midgley

Corporate Finance
James A. Brickley and Clifford W. Smith Jr

U.S. Federal Securities Law
Thomas Lee Hazen

Cybersecurity Law
David P. Fidler

Advanced Introduction to

Cybersecurity Law

DAVID P. FIDLER
*Senior Fellow for Cybersecurity and Global Health, Council
on Foreign Relations, USA*

Elgar Advanced Introductions

 Edward Elgar
PUBLISHING

Cheltenham, UK • Northampton, MA, USA

Published by
Edward Elgar Publishing Limited
The Lypiatts
15 Lansdown Road
Cheltenham
Glos GL50 2JA
UK

Edward Elgar Publishing, Inc.
William Pratt House
9 Dewey Court
Northampton
Massachusetts 01060
USA

A catalogue record for this book
is available from the British Library

Library of Congress Control Number: 2022934389

This book is available electronically on Elgar Advanced Introductions: Law
(www.advancedintros.com)

ISBN 978 1 80088 334 5 (cased)
ISBN 978 1 80088 336 9 (paperback)
ISBN 978 1 80088 335 2 (eBook)

Printed and bound in Great Britain by TJ Books Limited, Padstow, Cornwall

Contents

Figures

Tables

About the author

David P. Fidler is a senior fellow for cybersecurity and global health at the Council on Foreign Relations, USA. At CFR, he has contributed to *Net Politics*, the blog of CFR's Digital and Cyberspace Policy Program and written reports on cybersecurity issues, including "Cybersecurity and the New Era of Space Activities," *CFR Cyber Brief* (April 2018). He served as the chair of the International Law Association Study Group on Cybersecurity, Terrorism, and International Law (2014-16). He edited and contributed to *The Snowden Reader* (Indiana University Press, 2015). His recent publications include "Cyberspace and Human Rights,"

in *Research Handbook on International Law and Cyberspace*, 2nd ed. (Nicholas Tsagourias and Russell Buchan, eds.) (Edward Elgar, 2021), 130-51; "Foreign Election Interference and Open-Source Anarchy," in *Defending Democracies: Combating Foreign Election Interference in the Digital Age* (Jens David Ohlin and Duncan Hollis, eds.) (Oxford University Press, 2021), 293-313; and "SolarWinds and Microsoft Exchange: Hacks Wrapped in a Cybersecurity Dilemma Inside a Cyberspace Crisis," *Georgetown Journal of International Affairs* (April 2021). He holds degrees in law from Harvard Law School and the University of Oxford and in international relations from the University of Oxford.

Preface

In the late 1990s, concerns about 'non-lethal' weapons introduced me to the potential weaponization of internet-linked digital technologies. Initially, the possible development of other types of 'non-lethal' weapons preoccupied my attention, but, in the first decade of the new century, the significance of what came to be called 'cybersecurity' became more apparent. Governments began to grapple with cybercrime, terrorist use of the internet, cyber espionage, and the military potential of cyber technologies. But it was the Stuxnet operation exposed in 2010 that crystallized for me the policy and legal challenges that cybersecurity threats posed to governments, economies, societies, and individuals. Thereafter, cybersecurity became a core part of my endeavours as a professor at the Indiana University Maurer School of Law and my think-tank work with the Council on Foreign Relations.

This book derives from the materials I developed in teaching Cybersecurity Law and Policy for nearly a decade. As such, it benefits from the changes I made to my approach from interacting with students, learning from colleagues, and analysing the policy and legal implications of cybersecurity incidents and developments at home and abroad. In keeping with the purpose of *Elgar Advanced Introductions*, the book provides an accessible framework for understanding the field of cybersecurity and concise analysis of domestic and international law concerning each topic within the framework. The book also evaluates whether domestic and international law are proving effective against cybersecurity threats and identifies policy shifts made, and proposals offered, to improve cybersecurity within and among nations.

Given the diversity of national legal systems, the book's sections on domestic law focus on patterns discernible across countries that arise from how governments deal with cybersecurity threats. Examples from various countries are given, but the sections on domestic law primarily provide a roadmap for guiding more detailed study of how domestic legal systems handle cybersecurity challenges.

By contrast, international law provides an overarching set of rules that applies to the interactions of all states, which permits more uniformity in analysing how states use international law in addressing cybersecurity problems. However, international law reflects a different kind of diversity. On some problems, such as cybercrime, states have developed many international legal instruments. In some areas of cybersecurity, such as armed conflict, countries rely on international law developed before the internet and cyberspace became global phenomena. On yet other issues, such as cyber espionage, little, if any, international law exists. In terms of general international legal rules, such as on sovereignty and non-intervention in the domestic affairs of other states, states agree that such rules apply in cyberspace but prove reticent to clarify how they apply to features or consequences of cyber operations.

As an advanced introduction, the book does not systematically cite the scholarship and policy writing on cybersecurity. Much of this analytical work dissects cybersecurity events, challenges traditional perspectives on cybersecurity, and offers new ways to think about this field. This dynamic has been particularly interesting, for example, in connection with international law and cyber espionage. The book identifies prominent cybersecurity incidents, new policy perspectives, and leading legal reform ideas to prime the reader's exploration of additional material on specific cybersecurity episodes and different ways of countering cybersecurity threats. Where relevant, I point readers to chapters in the *Research Handbook on International Law and Cyberspace* (Edward Elgar, 2nd edn, 2021) to assist deeper study of issues raised in this book.

The book's final chapter summarizes the past 20 years in cybersecurity policy and law and ponders the challenges the next decade might bring. Looking backward and peering ahead are sobering exercises. Past efforts have proved less effective than hoped. Future actions must navigate more difficult national and international environments, including the return of balance-of-power politics to the international system. What emerges in this darker context remains to be seen. But a decade from now, an advanced introduction to cybersecurity law will likely look different to the one in your hands because you, perhaps, helped chart a new course for an area of policy and law that will only become more important with each passing day.

David P. Fidler
Clarendon Hills, Illinois, USA
15 October 2021

Post script

The Russian invasion of Ukraine in February 2022 occurred after this book's production process was completed. The armed conflict between Russia and Ukraine involved military kinetic and cyber operations and provides an important episode relevant to the analysis in Chapter 6.--D.P.F.

Abbreviations

art.	article in a legal document
CBMs	confidence-building measures
CIP	critical-infrastructure protection
COE	Council of Europe
DDoS	distributed denial of service
DNS	Domain Name System
EU	European Union
Europol	European Law Enforcement Agency
FISA	Foreign Intelligence Surveillance Act
ICANN	Internet Corporation for Assigned Names and Numbers
ICC	International Criminal Court
ICCPR	International Covenant on Civil and Political Rights
ICRC	International Committee of the Red Cross
ICT	information and communication technology
IETF	Internet Engineering Task Force
IGF	Internet Governance Forum
IHL	international humanitarian law
ITRs	International Telecommunication Regulations
ITU	International Telecommunication Union
MLAT	mutual legal assistance treaty
NATO	North Atlantic Treaty Organization
para.	paragraph in a document

R2P	responsibility to protect
sec.	section in a document
Tallinn Manual 2.0	*Tallinn Manual 2.0 on the International Law Applicable to Cyber Operations*
TCP/IP	Transmission Control Protocol/Internet Protocol
TRIPS	WTO Agreement on Trade-Related Aspects of Intellectual Property Rights
UK	United Kingdom
UN	United Nations
UNGGE	UN Group of Governmental Experts on Developments in the Field of Information and Telecommunications in the Context of International Security
US	United States
USC	United States Code
USMCA	United States–Mexico–Canada Agreement
VEP	vulnerabilities equities process
WTO	World Trade Organization

PART I

Background for cybersecurity law

1 Introduction: Cybersecurity and cybersecurity law

1.1 Defining cybersecurity

Cybersecurity has become one of the most important, fast-moving, and controversial areas in national and international politics. Ever-increasing political, economic, and social dependency on internet-linked digital technologies creates national and international security threats that governments struggle to counter. Despite attempts to mitigate them, the scale, intensity, speed, and seriousness of cybersecurity threats continue to grow. Ongoing innovation in information and communication technologies (ICTs) increases the importance of cyberspace, deepens reliance on such technologies, and heightens cybersecurity risks.

The persistence and seriousness of cybersecurity threats often leave the impression that cyberspace is a lawless place. This 'wild west' image ignores that governments extensively use policy and law in responding to cybersecurity threats. Cybersecurity policy addresses threats to sovereignty, security, prosperity, and liberty when countries, companies, civil society, and citizens are dependent on cyber technologies. This book explores the domestic and international law developed and applied to support cybersecurity policies.

Cybersecurity law encompasses domestic and international legal rules created for specific threats, such as cybercrime, as well as rules adopted for other purposes that apply in cyberspace, such as the law of armed conflict. The legal rules cover how the major categories of national security threats

– crime, terrorism, espionage, and war – arise in cyberspace. The rules reflect how governments:

- Prevent, protect against, respond to, and deter threats to digital information, software, hardware, services, and networks created by state and non-state actor use of ICTs; and
- Exploit digital information, software, hardware, services, and networks for law enforcement and national security purposes, including electronic surveillance, counterterrorism, espionage, and military operations.

These 'defensive' and 'offensive' activities define cybersecurity for policy and legal purposes. Despite the attention paid to cyber threats, no consensus definition of 'cybersecurity' exists. This problem arises, in part, from disagreements about what 'cyber' and 'security' mean. At its core, cybersecurity merges technological and political concerns created by how state and non-state actors use interlinked digital technologies to defend or damage resources, services, and activities important in the life of nations. The actual and potential damage cyber threats can inflict on governments, economies, societies, and individuals makes cybersecurity a national security priority for every country.

Under this definition of cybersecurity, the target, payload, vector, and impact of defensive and offensive activities are centred on ICTs. The targets are cyber based, including stored data, software programmes, computers, and information and communication networks. The means used to hit targets involve cyber payloads and vectors, such as delivering malware into a network through electronic mail. The direct impact on targets is cyber centric and includes compromising digital information, manipulating software, disrupting services, exploiting networks, and damaging hardware and computer-operated devices.

The direct impact might produce non-cyber consequences, including financial costs incurred to purge malware, the national security damage caused by the theft of classified information, and the physical destruction of computer-controlled machinery. In addition, the direct consequences of cyber operations might serve non-cyber purposes, such as gaining competitive advantages in global markets by stealing commercial information, disrupting democratic processes by hacking into voting systems, and prevailing in armed conflict by launching military cyberattacks.

This book's definition of cybersecurity also covers use of ICTs to counter conventional crime, terrorism, espionage, and military threats. Governments exploit ICTs to conduct electronic surveillance for law enforcement, counterterrorism, espionage, counterintelligence, and military purposes. Such surveillance can focus on cyber capabilities, such as an adversary's military information systems, or on non-cyber threats, such as terrorists preparing kinetic attacks. Electronic surveillance can undermine the security of cyber-based systems used by governments, corporations, and citizens, even when the law authorizes the surveillance for a legitimate purpose, as happens when law-enforcement agencies engage in lawful hacking.

This framing of cybersecurity means that not every policy issue and national security threat involving ICTs is a cybersecurity problem. For example, transnational criminal organizations sell counterfeit pharmaceuticals online. Terrorists use the internet to spread propaganda. Companies use digital information from customers in ways that create privacy concerns. Governments spread disinformation through social media to interfere in the domestic politics of adversary states. Intelligence agents use electronic mail and text messaging to recruit people to spy against their governments. Military forces integrate digital command, control, and communication networks to support conventional military operations. These examples illustrate that many uses of ICTs create policy, legal, and national security problems that are not cybersecurity threats.[1]

The purpose of defining cybersecurity is to provide parameters for analysing how domestic and international law operate in this policy area. However, most definitions break down when real-world complexities challenge aspirations for analytical clarity and precision. The cyber aspects of national security policy are much broader than this book's definition of cybersecurity. The growing dependence on ICTs at every level of society makes drawing clear lines between 'cybersecurity' and 'cyberspace and national security' increasingly hard.

---

[1]   For the range of international legal issues associated with cyberspace, see Nicholas Tsagourias and Russell Buchan, eds, *Research Handbook on International Law and Cyberspace* (Edward Elgar, 2nd edn, 2021) [hereinafter *Research Handbook on International Law and Cyberspace*].

Two examples of blurred lines involve information operations. The *Oxford Statement on International Law Protections in Cyberspace: The Regulation of Information Operations and Activities* (2021) defined 'information operations' as 'any deployment of digital resources for cognitive purposes to change or reinforce attitudes or behaviours of the targeted audience'. In attempting to create a caliphate in Iraq and Syria in the mid-2010s, the Islamic State terrorist group used social media to spread propaganda, recruit supporters, radicalize adherents, and obtain funds. These actions were not cybersecurity issues because the Islamic State simply used social media platforms rather than gaining unauthorized access and manipulating them. Even so, the Islamic State's online activities contributed to the national security threat the group posed to many countries. In waging armed conflict against the Islamic State, several countries supported conventional military actions with cyber operations against the group's online activities and capabilities. These offensive military operations fall within the scope of cybersecurity policy and law (see Chapter 6).

The second example comes from information operations mounted by authoritarian states against elections in democratic countries.[2] These campaigns can, but do not necessarily, involve compromising computers, services, networks, or digital data. During the 2016 election in the United States, Russian intelligence agencies hacked into the computer networks of the Democratic National Committee, exfiltrated information, and leaked it to interfere with the election campaign. More frequently, information operations designed to meddle in democratic processes are not cybersecurity threats because they disseminate disinformation on social media to exacerbate political divisions within countries and discredit the democratic process. In 2018, the United States engaged in offensive cyber operations to disrupt Russian disinformation campaigns designed to meddle in US elections (see Chapter 6).

Definitions also reveal problems that have nothing to do with analytical clarity. China and Russia prefer using the term 'information security' rather than 'cybersecurity', even when the Chinese and Russian governments are talking about the same threats as other states, such as cyber-

---

[2]   On this problem, see Duncan B. Hollis and Jens David Ohlin, eds, *Defending Democracies: Combatting Foreign Election Interference in a Digital Age* (OUP, 2021); and the *Oxford Statement on International Law Protections against Foreign Electoral Interference through Digital Means* (2020).

crime. However, the preference for information security highlights that China and Russia have different national security interests, especially their fear of political opponents using the internet to challenge government policies and power. This difference between cybersecurity and information security informs the 'internet freedom' versus 'internet sovereignty' debate about internet governance (see Chapter 2). This debate has important implications for cybersecurity, but it is not a debate about cybersecurity.

Drawing analytical lines between cybersecurity and the broader spectrum of national security challenges associated with cyberspace does not, and should not, minimize the importance of those challenges. As the Islamic State example illustrates, terrorist exploitation of the internet to spread propaganda, radicalize adherents, and raise funds has – to date – been a bigger national security problem than terrorists launching cyberattacks to disrupt or damage the critical infrastructure of countries.

Even with these definitional caveats, the behaviour of states and non-state actors makes cybersecurity a growing concern for individuals, corporations, non-governmental organizations, societies, and governments. Whether all the attention and resources devoted to cybersecurity has produced better cybersecurity remains questionable, and no easy policy or legal answers exist.

1.2   Cybersecurity law: Overview of the book

This book provides an advanced introduction to how governments use law in responding to cybersecurity threats and in taking actions that have cybersecurity consequences.[3] In each context, domestic and international law play important roles in shaping policy approaches, facilitating policy implementation, and evaluating the legitimacy and effectiveness of policy actions.[4] The analysis begins with background material on the relation-

---

[3]   For a broader look at the relationship between law and cyberspace, see Nicholas Tsagourias, 'The Legal Status of Cyberspace: Sovereignty Redux?', in *Research Handbook on International Law and Cyberspace*, 9–31.

[4]   The diversity of national legal systems, combined with differences in how governments use domestic law to address cybersecurity, creates challenges

ships between cyberspace, security, and law (Chapter 2). The chapter describes how the technological innovations creating the internet have produced security concerns that governments address through cybersecurity policy. The chapter explores how cybersecurity policy relates to internet governance and informs how states have crafted different governance approaches for cybersecurity. The background material ends with analysis of the functions of law in cyberspace, how countries have used law in addressing innovation in ICTs, and the patterns that developed as governments used domestic and international law for cybersecurity purposes.

The next four chapters address the main analytical categories of cybersecurity threats – crime (Chapter 3), terrorism (Chapter 4), espionage (Chapter 5), and armed conflict (Chapter 6). These categories reflect traditional policy frameworks for security threats that governments have used in responding to cybersecurity challenges. As distinct categories, the law applicable to crime, terrorism, espionage, and armed conflict in cyberspace differs, and the chapters analyse the domestic and international legal rules developed for each cyber-threat category.

However, using these traditional threat categories in the cybersecurity context is not without problems. For example, categorizing a cyber incident as criminal in nature means applying criminal law to the perpetrator. Governments intend criminal sanctions to deter criminal behaviour by proscribing and punishing criminal acts, but the relentless growth of cybercrime globally suggests that criminal law does not create much of a deterrent (Chapter 3). Categorizing a cyber incident as espionage encounters a different problem. International law does not prohibit espionage, and domestic laws criminalizing espionage have never deterred governments from spying on each other (Chapter 5). Further, using these cyber-threat categories tends to be reactive because this approach involves identifying policy and legal responses after cyber incidents have occurred rather than protecting against or preventing cyber threats.

Given problems the cyber-threat approach encounters, policymakers have explored other ways to strengthen cybersecurity, such as building

---

for analysing domestic cybersecurity laws. By contrast, international law applicable to cybersecurity affects all countries, which permits analysis of rules that apply across the international system.

better cyber defences whatever the nature of a cyber threat. This 'all hazards' approach seeks to 'harden the target' by protecting cyber systems from any cyber operation emanating from any source undertaken for any reason. Improving cyber defences can prevent cyberattacks from succeeding, limit the damage they cause, and facilitate faster recovery from attacks. Strong cyber defences can deter state and non-state actors from conducting cyber operations by creating 'deterrence by denial'. The cyber-defence strategy involves different legal issues than those arising under the cyber-threat approach.

However, the cyber-defence approach also has problems. 'Harden the target' actions can generate benefits, but governments, corporations, non-governmental organizations, and individuals often underinvest in, or lack the resources and technological capabilities to strengthen, cyber defences. The cyber-defence approach also faces difficulties in many countries because much of the cyber infrastructure is under private-sector control. Weak private-sector cybersecurity measures continue to be a concern, especially with cyber-enabled critical infrastructure, such as electricity, water, and medical services. How to use domestic and international law effectively to address these vulnerabilities remains a work in progress. In addition, many experts believe that the offence has too many advantages over the defence in cyberspace, which limits what cyber defences can achieve, especially against highly capable states or sophisticated non-state actors.

Scepticism about the cyber-threat and cyber-defence approaches has stimulated interest in achieving more robust cyber deterrence – the building of 'full spectrum' defensive and offensive cyber capabilities to deter and, when necessary, punish and defeat adversaries. This approach emphasizes 'deterrence by punishment', achieved by credible threats to use cyber means to impose disproportionate costs on adversaries that undertake certain cyber actions. For such threats to be credible, those issuing them must possess the offensive cyber capabilities to carry out the threats. This requirement means that the cyber-deterrence approach has gained more prominence in countries that can afford to build, maintain, and operate such offensive capabilities. Pursuing cyber deterrence generates its own set of legal issues,[5] which differ from the legal features of the

---

[5]   See, e.g., Eric Myjer, 'Some Thoughts on Cyber Deterrence and Public International Law', in *Research Handbook on International Law and Cyberspace*, 365–85.

cyber-threat and cyber-defence strategies. Even though cyber deterrence has gained increased policy attention, whether it can be an effective cyber-security strategy remains controversial for legal and other reasons.

Identifying the cyber-threat, cyber-defence, and cyber-deterrence approaches highlights how cybersecurity policy has evolved. In policy and law, these strategies can operate independently and in mutually supportive ways. For example, strengthening cybersecurity in critical infrastructure sectors, such as electrical utilities, can involve criminalizing unauthorized cyber operations against such infrastructure, strengthening the cyber defences of power-generation facilities, and deterring cyberat-tacks against such facilities by threatening retaliatory cyber punishment against those launching such attacks. As needed, the chapters in this book will analyse the legal features of the cyber-threat, cyber-defence, and cyber-deterrence approaches as they arise within the four categories of national security threats.

The structure of Chapters 3 to 6 is the same. Each provides an overview of the cybersecurity problem in question followed by analysis of the domes-tic and international legal topics, issues, and challenges that arise for that problem. This approach facilitates analysis of which rules apply, how they apply, what legal consequences arise from violations, and why the rules encounter problems that undermine the effectiveness of cybersecurity strategies.

In terms of applicable law, the chapters discuss rules developed before cybersecurity became a policy priority and explore how such 'legacy' laws work in the context of cybersecurity. For example, the international law on sovereignty supports the development of domestic cybercrime laws, creates problems for international cooperation on cybercrime, and factors into why transnational criminal organizations often engage in cybercrime with near impunity (Chapter 3). The law of armed conflict developed to address increasingly violent, destructive, and lethal kinetic warfare, so the less violent, destructive, and lethal consequences that cyber weapons can produce present challenges for this law (Chapter 6). In assessing how applicable laws work, the chapters highlight legal problems that arise in each policy category.

Assessing whether cyber activities have violated laws also raises the related issues of attribution and accountability. Domestic law and international law have rules that determine when state or non-state actors can be held responsible for illegal acts. For example, a cyber operation might have violated the international law on the use of force, but the evidence might be insufficient to attribute that violation to a specific state under the international law on state responsibility. Attribution is a challenge in cybersecurity because perpetrators can manipulate technologies to disguise the source of cyber operations. This problem can create headaches because domestic and international law have demanding rules on attribution that determine when punishment or countermeasures can be applied to alleged perpetrators.

The final chapter considers the challenges that cybersecurity policy and law face in the future (Chapter 7). Technological developments continue to affect cybersecurity, including 5G wireless telecommunication, blockchain technology, artificial intelligence, cryptocurrencies, and quantum computing. Politically, democracies are on the defensive – a change from the post-Cold War period when democracy as a form of government and internet freedom as a vision of cyberspace were ascendant. Deep divisions and hyper-partisanship in US politics create challenges for the United States to demonstrate the international leadership on cyberspace and cybersecurity it provided for over 20 years. Led by China and Russia, authoritarian states are exploiting this situation by adopting and promoting 'digital authoritarianism'.[6] The assertiveness of China and Russia, along with the troubles afflicting the United States and the community of democracies, signals that the balance of power in the international system has shifted. The return of technological, ideological, and geopolitical competition to international relations means that cyberspace and its associated technologies will be fertile sources of controversy, confrontation, coercion, and conflict over the next decade. In this environment, the prospects for more effective use of domestic and international law against cybersecurity threats do not look promising.

---

[6]   See Freedom House, *Freedom on the Net 2018: The Rise of Digital Authoritarianism* (November 2018); and Steven Feldstein, *The Rise of Digital Repression: How Technology is Reshaping Power, Politics, and Resistance* (OUP, 2021).

2   Cyberspace, security, and law

The domestic and international law developed for cybersecurity primarily emerged because of the internet, perhaps the most transformative ICT ever invented. Domestic and international politics have shaped, and continue to influence, the internet's evolution. These political dimensions inform how the internet makes 'cyberspace' a realm of political activity and inform what 'security' in cyberspace means. How countries, companies, civil society, and citizens use the internet reflects governance strategies and legal frameworks that structure and regulate what happens in cyberspace, including efforts to achieve cybersecurity.

This chapter explores the technological, political, and legal contexts that affect how governments use domestic and international law for cybersecurity. The analysis begins by examining what security in cyberspace involves, which requires understanding perspectives on what the internet, cyberspace, and security mean (Section 2.1). The chapter then looks at how the internet is governed (Section 2.2) and how internet governance relates to the ways in which states and non-state actors attempt to govern cybersecurity (Section 2.3). The chapter concludes by unpacking the roles of domestic and international law in cybersecurity governance (Section 2.4).

2.1   What is 'security' in 'cyberspace'?

2.1.1   What is the 'internet'?

Technological innovation that facilitates communications and information sharing has a long history, including the printing press, telegraph, telephony, radio, television, satellites, and the internet. Individually and collectively, such inventions have had significant political, economic, and legal consequences within and among nations. For example, the creation of the telegraph prompted states to establish the International Telegraph Union in 1865, one of the earliest international organizations. However, across history, no technological innovation for communications and information sharing has had the impact the internet has achieved.

One way to sense this impact is to appreciate how the internet has revolutionized communications previously conducted through older technologies. People use the internet to publish digital books, send electronic messages, engage in person-to-person telephony, listen to the radio, participate in video meetings, and watch recorded and live video broadcasts. The internet affects the use of satellites, including the deployment of thousands of small, networked satellites designed to boost global internet access. The internet is the most multi-functional ICT ever invented. The nature, interoperability, and scalability of its component technologies mean the internet links billions of people around the world – connectivity and accessibility no previous technology achieved. The internet is a technology of versatile capabilities and mass participation.

The internet facilitates transmission of information through a network that links digital technologies, such as computers and mobile devices. The network connects such technologies through a suite of standard communication protocols – known as the Transmission Control Protocol/Internet Protocol (TCP/IP). Originally developed in the early 1970s, these protocols permit the network to have an 'open-architecture', meaning that different kinds of devices can communicate without requiring each device to have identical hardware and software. The standard protocols permit the transmission of information by 'packet switching', which breaks digital data into 'packets' that the protocols route over different parts of the network to the eventual destination, where the packets are reassembled. The internet does not rely on direct end-to-end connections used to transmit information over circuits, as happened, for example, with analogue telephony.

Interoperable standard protocols operating in an open-architecture network required additional innovations to achieve scale in adoption and accessibility. The development of the Domain Name System in 1983 permitted the internet to achieve greater scale by harmonizing internet addresses and resolving problems as the number of addresses increased.

In 1993, software for the World Wide Web was made freely available. Through its hypertext transfer protocol (HTTP), universal resource locators (URLs), and hypertext markup language (HTML), the 'web' made the internet more accessible and contributed to the increase in internet use around the world.

Other innovations played a role in the internet's success. In particular, the progress made in the capacity, speed, capabilities, and affordability of mainframe, desktop, and portable computers spread access to internet-capable digital technologies far and wide. Greater access and use of the internet through better computers generated a feedback loop in which the internet influenced the creation of new technologies, such as smart phones and tablet devices. The internet also produced incentives to connect products, from cars to refrigerators, to the web, creating the 'internet of things'.

2.1.2   What is 'cyberspace'?

As a technology, the internet is magnificent. But the internet has always been more than a technological achievement. The origins of research that produced the internet began in the United States during the Cold War with funding from the US Department of Defense. These origins link the internet's evolution with geopolitical, national security, and military strategies designed to help the United States counter the threat posed by the Soviet Union. The Cold War ended contemporaneously with the advent of the technological innovations that triggered global internet access and use. The convergence of these geopolitical and technological transformations made people think about the internet as more than just another technology. Instead, the internet created a new realm of political, economic, and social behaviour in 'cyberspace'.

What cyberspace is, or should be, has stimulated diverse perspectives. An early, iconic vision came from John Perry Barlow's *A Declaration of the Independence of Cyberspace* (1996), which portrays cyberspace as a place that individuals – not governments – control. 'We are forming our own Social Contract', the declaration proclaimed, and '[t]his governance will arise according to the conditions of our world', not the world of physical borders that governments police. In other perspectives, cyberspace reflects and promotes the values of liberal, free-market democracies, especially individual liberty, freedom of expression, and self-government.

Less sanguine views cautioned that cyberspace, like all political spaces, is a contested realm that does not favour any ideology or governmental system.

Decades of debates reveal that concepts of cyberspace reflect how ideas and power shift within and among countries. The early, optimistic perspectives on cyberspace dominated in the aftermath of the triumph of liberal democracies in the Cold War. More pessimistic interpretations appeared as non-democratic countries, led by China and Russia, subjected the internet to sovereignty and cyberspace to government control, producing concerns that the global internet was becoming a 'splinternet'. The rise of digital authoritarianism suggests that cyberspace is a fertile place for non-democratic power and ideas at a time when, in democracies, cyberspace often looks like a cesspool of disinformation, racism, misogyny, conspiracy theories, incivility, distrust of public institutions, corporate monopoly power, and a stimulant of violence. Fears that cyberspace threatens democracy and favours authoritarianism have become prominent as balance-of-power politics, especially between the United States and China, have returned to the international system, ending the period of US hegemony.

This pattern in perspectives on cyberspace is important for understanding the development of cybersecurity policy. In the initial post-Cold War years, democracies prioritized non-traditional security threats from terrorists and criminals rather than from states. At that time, democracies, benefiting from the collapse of the Soviet Union and the hegemonic power of the United States, did not face geopolitical threats. As China and Russia emerged as rival states, traditional national security concerns in the intelligence and military realms gained more prominence. Governments began to perceive cyberspace as a competitive, dangerous domain of espionage, covert action, and armed conflict among states. The transition from US hegemony to a balance-of-power system has further elevated traditional national security worries in policy thinking about cyberspace and cybersecurity.

2.1.3   What is 'security'?

Understanding cybersecurity requires exploring not only 'cyber' but also 'security'. What constitutes security for individuals, societies, and countries has been debated for centuries. In *The Leviathan* (1651), Thomas

Hobbes focused on the threat that the anarchical state of nature created for each individual's life and asserted that a government must be established to impose and maintain order. Security among nations, Immanuel Kant argued in *Perpetual Peace: A Philosophical Sketch* (1795), happens when all states are democratic republics. In *The Communist Manifesto* (1848), Karl Marx and Friedrich Engels claimed that individual and international security will occur only when capitalism's collapse ushers in communism. Across such diverse perspectives flow ideas of human, national, and international security.

As a concept rooted in technology, cybersecurity focuses on vulnerabilities in cyber technologies that make internet-facilitated activities insecure for individuals, economies, societies, and governments. These technical vulnerabilities in software, devices, and networked systems create risks of unauthorized access and use that can result in, among other things, fraudulent use of an individual's identity, theft of a company's intellectual property, disruption of a society's critical infrastructure, exposure of a government's secrets, or degradation of a country's military capabilities. Vulnerabilities range from poor password practices by users to sophisticated, remote, and covert exploitation of 'bugs' in software. Ever-greater dependence on cyber technologies magnifies the policy impact that these vulnerabilities have, such that cybersecurity touches individual, economic, national, and global security concerns.

This broad scope forces cybersecurity analysis to grapple with larger concepts of security, such as national security, that influence what cybersecurity means for reasons not centred on cyber technologies. For example, US national security policy has long sought to achieve unrivalled military capabilities to defend against, deter, and defeat military threats from adversary states on land, at sea, in the air, and in outer space. This posture informs the US government's thinking about cyberspace as a war-fighting domain and its desire to develop powerful, offensive military cyber capabilities. Other countries have responded in kind to avoid being vulnerable to US cyber power. The resulting 'militarization' of cyberspace has exacerbated cybersecurity problems around the world. In a context of geopolitical competition, cyber actions and reactions become absorbed in the larger strategic contest for power and influence, which Hobbes described as states being in the 'posture of war' with 'their weapons pointing and their eyes fixed on one another' and with 'continual spies upon their neighbours' (*The Leviathan*, chap. XIII).

In addition, what individual, economic, and national security means differs across nations, especially as between democratic and authoritarian states and high-income and low-income countries. Formulation of national security strategies in democracies constantly faces questions about the limits of the government's national security powers *vis-à-vis* the rights of citizens and the interests of private-sector activities. Authoritarian governments generally recognize no limits to their national security powers within their borders. These tendencies in democratic and authoritarian states appear in cybersecurity policy. Democracies grapple with how their governments conduct domestic electronic surveillance for cybersecurity purposes and regulate the private sector to combat cyber-crime and economic cyber espionage.[1] By contrast, China imposes an internet 'firewall', conducts extensive electronic surveillance, and censors online activities in the interests of national security.

Differences between democracies and authoritarian states also appear in how many authoritarian governments use 'information security' or 'cyberspace security' rather than cybersecurity as an organizing concept. A treaty on information security among the authoritarian states in the Shanghai Cooperation Organization covers not only vulnerabilities in cyber technologies but also the risks that the content of online information creates for national security. Under the rubric of information or cyberspace security, authoritarian governments censor political speech that they claim threatens social order. The spread of digital authoritarianism includes governments prohibiting and punishing speech of political opponents as sedition, terrorism, disinformation, or 'fake news'. The scope of information or cyberspace security is broader than cybersecurity as defined in this book, but the difference underscores that countries do not see eye-to-eye on the security challenges created by the use of cyber technologies.

Many countries have adopted national cyberspace strategies, which facilitates comparative analysis of different national security approaches to cyber-related problems.[2] These documents typically address the issues that this book uses to define cybersecurity, and approaches for managing

---

[1]   Chapters 3, 4, and 5 explore how governments use law to align cybersecurity needs with individual rights and private-sector interests.
[2]   For national cyber strategies, see the NATO Cooperative Cyber Defence Centre of Excellence's 'Strategy and Governance' online database.

these issues frequently emphasize common themes, such as the importance of international cooperation on cybercrime and strengthening national cyber defences within the government, critical infrastructure, private sector, and non-governmental organizations. However, many strategies do not discuss the cyber activities of intelligence agencies and military forces, which leaves out critical cybersecurity sectors, issues, and threats. Some countries, including the United States, have started to increase the transparency of their intelligence and military cyber policies for several reasons, including to support governmental accountability at home and bolster cyber deterrence abroad.

2.2   What is internet governance?

Whatever the issue, governments adopt and implement policies within governance structures and processes that allocate authority and resources and impose limits on the exercise of political power. Understanding the governance challenges and controversies in cybersecurity requires examining governance of the internet and cybersecurity problems that arise with the use of interconnected cyber technologies. Internet governance is a broad topic that implicates more than cybersecurity, but the internet's centrality to the nature of cybersecurity problems makes internet governance important for the specific topic of cybersecurity governance (Section 2.3).

As a preliminary matter, governance is not the same thing as government. Certainly, the exercise of governmental authority produces governance, but governance happens in the absence of a government or governmental mandates. At the international level, no world government exists, yet states govern their interactions through international law, voluntary regimes, non-binding norms, and political mechanisms, such as the balance of power. Similarly, governance within a state often involves more than law. For example, without any government mandate, corporations and non-governmental organizations provide goods and services that meet human needs and help maintain social order.

The internet did not happen without governance – people and institutions making decisions about how the internet would develop and operate. Initially, internet governance was the province of the small number of researchers in a few countries who created the technologies and strategies that made the internet work. As internet use grew, internet governance accommodated larger, more diverse, and globally disseminated communities. In this transition, questions about how the internet is governed, and by whom, became more frequent and contentious. For this book's purposes, the most important controversies have been about whether internet governance should (1) happen through a multi-stakeholder or intergovernmental process; and (2) address cybersecurity threats. Boiled down, these controversies focus on who or what exercises political power concerning the internet, and for what purposes such power is exercised.

The internet is the product of governance processes that governments and intergovernmental organizations have not controlled. The processes have been multi-stakeholder endeavours, meaning that people and bodies from academia, the private sector, civil society, and governments collaborate in making the internet work. The Internet Engineering Task Force (IETF) has established, published, and maintained the protocols that make the global TCP/IP network function. The IETF sets internet protocols by involving 'anyone who wants to participate ... through an organization that has no formal legal existence or fixed place of operation' and which acts 'only when there is consensus among everybody involved that it should be so'.[3]

The IETF's protocols are not mandatory or legally binding, but the internet operates for billions of users because the IETF standards are adopted and implemented globally. Similarly, governance of internet addresses through the Domain Name System (DNS) has happened through a multi-stakeholder process, which the Internet Corporation for Assigned Names and Numbers (ICANN), a non-governmental organization, manages. ICANN oversees the DNS by, among other things, resolving disputes over domain names and expanding the DNS through adoption of new generic, top-level domain names.

The way internet governance emerged differed from how governance of earlier innovations – such as the telegraph, telephony, and radio – evolved. As noted earlier, states decided in the nineteenth century to develop international standards for the telegraph through an intergovern-

---

[3]   David G. Post, *In Search of Jefferson's Moose: Notes on the State of Cyberspace* (OUP, 2009), 134.

mental organization, the International Telegraph Union. States expanded the union's remit to include telephony and radio communications and renamed it the International Telecommunication Union (ITU) in 1932 to reflect its broader agenda. In establishing the ITU and creating international standards, states used international law in the form of legally binding treaties. The governance approach used for these earlier breakthrough technologies was intergovernmental and based on international legal agreements.

The internet became a global phenomenon outside the ITU and without treaties establishing the governance processes and international standards for it. Such different governance for the internet was not universally celebrated. Several countries, including China and Russia, expressed concerns that multi-stakeholder governance masked the power that the United States wielded over the internet and the threat that such power created for sovereignty and national security.[4] These concerns fuelled efforts to make internet governance more intergovernmental through the United Nations (UN).[5]

The UN convened the World Summit on the Information Society in the early 2000s, and disagreements about internet governance produced a compromise called the Internet Governance Forum (IGF). The IGF has had little, if any, impact on internet governance and has not transformed multi-stakeholder processes, including the IETF and ICANN. Countries favouring intergovernmental governance of the internet also pushed this agenda within the ITU. The conference convened in 2012 to revise an ITU treaty, the International Telecommunication Regulations (ITRs), ended in acrimony over disagreements between countries backing

---

4   On Russian and Chinese perspectives, see Sergey Sayapin, 'Russian Approaches to International Law and Cyberspace', in Nicholas Tsagourias and Russell Buchan, eds, *Research Handbook on International Law and Cyberspace* (Edward Elgar, 2nd edn, 2021) [hereinafter *Research Handbook on International Law and Cyberspace*], 524–45; and Zhixiong Huang and Yaohui Ying, 'Chinese Approaches to Cyberspace Governance and International Law', in *Research Handbook on International Law and Cyberspace*, 546–62.

5   On the UN and cybersecurity, see Christian Henderson, 'The United Nations and the Regulation of Cyber-Security', in *Research Handbook on International Law and Cyberspace*, 581–613.

multi-stakeholder governance and nations seeking more intergovernmental governance.

Controversies about internet governance have also arisen at the domestic level. Generally, countries supportive of multi-stakeholder governance have championed internet freedom. Under this perspective, governments should govern the internet domestically in ways that support democracy, enable free markets, protect civil and political rights, and promote an open and global internet. States pushing for intergovernmental governance have embraced internet sovereignty or cyber sovereignty, under which the exercise of national sovereignty determines how the internet functions within a nation and among countries.

The 'internet freedom v. internet sovereignty' debate became increasingly contentious. China, Russia, and other proponents of internet sovereignty have imposed greater restrictions on domestic internet use and advanced the cause of intergovernmental governance of the internet. According to Freedom House's report on *Freedom on the Net 2020*, the growing strength of the internet sovereignty movement contributed to a decade-long decline in internet freedom around the world. Controversies within democracies over electronic surveillance by governments, online disinformation by citizens and foreign actors, and hate speech on social media have adversely affected efforts to advance internet freedom globally.

Among the issues it touches, the internet governance debate has involved cybersecurity. The focus on interoperable protocols and an open-architecture network in creating the internet paid little attention to security. This feature of the internet's development continued in how internet governance processes operated without sustained concern for cybersecurity. Even so, many democracies have opposed addressing cybersecurity within internet governance forums. The ITU conference in 2012 on revising the ITRs broke down, in part, because the United States would not agree to a provision requiring states parties to 'endeavour to ensure the security … of international telecommunication networks' (art. 5A). The United States did not believe the ITU or the ITRs were appropriate venues for addressing cybersecurity. Disagreements between democratic and authoritarian states about what security means in connection with the internet and cyberspace (Section 2.1.3) contributed to the controversy associated with revising the ITRs to include security concerns.

2.3   What is cybersecurity governance?

The nature, scale, and seriousness of cybersecurity threats have generated efforts to require and encourage state and non-state actors to adopt policies, practices, and behaviours to improve cybersecurity. This book's subsequent chapters examine how governments use domestic and international law to achieve better cybersecurity governance, but, as in other policy areas, governance activities in cybersecurity involve more than legal instruments and mechanisms. The use of legal rules and non-legal initiatives produces a mixture of activities designed to strengthen cybersecurity within and among nations. Domestically and internationally, cybersecurity governance reflects the development of 'regime complexes' – sets of overlapping strategies, processes, mechanisms, norms, rules, and measures that shape public and private efforts to address cybersecurity threats.

At the domestic level, private-sector enterprises are victims of cybercrime by criminal organizations and economic cyber espionage by foreign governments. Chapters 3 and 5 explore the criminal law that governments use to address these threats. However, states and non-state actors supplement the legal regimes with other governance mechanisms. For example, governments and corporations collaborate in the voluntary sharing of information to produce heightened situational awareness about threats in cyberspace. Without any legal obligation, companies use frameworks crafted through public-private partnerships to assess their cybersecurity risks and adopt better cybersecurity measures. Government agencies and corporations sponsor programmes, such as 'bug bounty' challenges, that encourage hackers to identify vulnerabilities in software and information systems as another way to improve cybersecurity. In policy terms, many non-legal governance regimes that operate domestically seek to help public and private actors strengthen cyber defences against threats from criminals and foreign governments.

At the international level, states seek to improve cybersecurity through governance strategies implemented in bilateral, regional, collective defence, and multilateral forums. Countries have crafted bilateral cybersecurity arrangements, as the United States has done with several countries. The European Union (EU), one of the leading regional institutions, has developed various cybersecurity initiatives, and other regional organizations have produced cybercrime treaties (Chapter 3). In the collective defence realm, the North Atlantic Treaty Organization (NATO) has worked to improve cyber-defence capabilities across the alliance.[6] The UN has sponsored efforts through which its member states have identified non-binding norms for responsible state behaviour in cyberspace.[7]

Efforts within the EU, NATO, and the UN illustrate the hybrid nature of international cybersecurity governance regimes. These and other international organizations operate under legally binding treaties, the provisions of which accommodate the development of legal and non-legal approaches to improving cybersecurity. As with domestic efforts, many international cybersecurity governance activities centre on helping countries improve national cyber defences through, for example, sharing information, strengthening communication and response capabilities, and providing technical assistance.

The number and diversity of regime complexes at the domestic and international levels are not evidence of the effectiveness of cybersecurity governance. The continuing need to shore up cyber defences against cybercrime and cyber espionage arises because domestic and international legal rules adopted for these threats have not provided much protection. This problem highlights the incentives in cybersecurity policy to supplement legal rules specific to the different cyber threats with building 'all hazards' cyber-defence capabilities (Chapter 1). Increasing interest in the cyber-deterrence approach also suggests that doubts exist about the effectiveness of efforts to bolster cyber defences against intelligence and military cyber threats posed by foreign governments. However, the governance context for cyber deterrence has been less clear because it involves intelligence and military capabilities and activities often kept secret. In addition, cyber deterrence is controversial because the premise that deterrence in cyberspace is possible remains hotly debated.

---

[6]   See, e.g., Steven Hill, 'NATO and the International Law of Cyber Defence', in *Research Handbook on International Law and Cyberspace*, 508–23.

[7]   On cyber norms, see Marja Lehto, 'The Rise of Cyber Norms', in *Research Handbook on International Law and Cyberspace*, 32–45.

2.4   What is the role of law in cybersecurity governance?

2.4.1   The functions of law and technological change

In all policy areas, law is used to authorize and constrain the exercise of political power. Constitutional law authorizes certain actors to exercise different powers (e.g., the legislature has the power to tax and spend). Constitutional law also constrains how governmental actors exercise their powers by, for example, protecting individual rights. Similarly, international law authorizes states to exercise political power by protecting territorial sovereignty and constrains how states exercise sovereignty in international relations by, for example, prohibiting intervention in the domestic affairs of other states. Law fulfils the same authorization and limitation functions in connection with cybersecurity governance.

However, the internet has generated questions about whether traditional conceptions of law work in cyberspace. A *Declaration of the Independence of Cyberspace* envisioned cyberspace as a political space in which governments did not make the law. Lawrence Lessig argued that 'code is law' because the software codes that run the internet 'regulate cyberspace as it is'.[8] The internet's global scope has created problems for fundamental international legal concepts, such as the allocation of jurisdiction in the international system. UN member states have struggled to reach consensus on how international law applies in cyberspace.

These and other examples illustrate that the internet has presented legal systems with an array of challenges. Over time, the novelty of these challenges has faded. Today, that governments make law for cyberspace is clear. Constraints on government law-making often arise from political choices not to regulate or from pre-internet rules, such as constitutional rights for individuals, rather than anything intrinsically different about cyber technologies. The software codes that run the internet do not regulate cyberspace, as a comparison between how cyberspace operates in democracies and authoritarian countries demonstrates. Countries have applied long-standing strategies for handling transnational problems, such as harmonization of domestic law through treaties, to address the jurisdictional issues that the internet has generated. The persistence of

---

[8]   Lawrence Lessig, *Code and Other Laws of Cyberspace* (Basic Books, 1999), 6.

traditional approaches means that states prefer how existing law structures the exercise of political power in response to cyberspace issues. Controversies about how international law applies in cyberspace arise from political competition for power among rival countries rather than any inadequacy of international law that cyber technologies uniquely reveal.

2.4.2   Domestic law and cybersecurity governance

In addition to adopting policies and implementing non-legal governance initiatives, governments have used domestic law to address cybersecurity challenges. Legal activity has occurred within each cyber-threat category – crime, terrorism, espionage, and armed conflict. Many countries have revised their criminal codes to reflect the cybercrime threat by adding new crimes and expanding law-enforcement authorities. Concerns that terrorists might launch cyberattacks against critical infrastructure led some countries to create legal regimes to protect against such attacks. In responding to increased public and private dependence on the internet, governments have revisited the legal powers and limits that apply to electronic surveillance undertaken by law enforcement, espionage conducted by intelligence agencies, and cyber operations executed by military forces.

Although domestic legal activities on cybersecurity cover much governance territory, legal action has often raised age-old questions that are anchored in the basic functions of law. What government actors have the legal authority to address cybersecurity challenges? Do government actors, such as law-enforcement agencies and military forces, have sufficient legal powers to respond to cybersecurity threats? Are new legal limits needed to protect individual rights, economic activities, and other interests and values when governments defend against cybersecurity threats or exploit cyber technologies for national security purposes? Do non-state actors, such as corporations, need more legal authority or protection to take cybersecurity actions, such as sharing cyber-threat information with government agencies or 'hacking back' against cybercriminals?

As the tension between internet freedom and internet sovereignty suggests, countries answer these and other legal questions differently depending on political ideology, the structure of governmental power, and the nature of domestic legal systems. The fragmentation of the internet – the splinternet phenomenon – arises largely from governments that want more sovereign control over cyberspace 'drawing national boundaries around the internet'.[9] Diversity and disharmony also appear among democracies on matters such as, for example, protection of an individual's right to privacy, regulation of the private sector to improve cyber defences, the scope of authority to conduct electronic surveillance, and the benefits of offensive military cyber operations.

Increasingly, democracies are responding to cybersecurity threats in ways that contribute to the splintering of the internet. The US effort to counter Chinese cyber espionage includes a strategy – the Clean Network Program – to prevent Chinese technology enterprises from supplying or servicing communication and information networks in the United States and other democracies. Advocates of an open, global internet criticized the program for fracturing the internet even more. The Chinese government countered with its own cybersecurity initiative that doubled down on its emphasis on sovereignty over internet activities. In this episode and others, democratic and authoritarian countries are increasingly exercising sovereign powers to draw geopolitical boundaries across cyberspace.

2.4.3   International law and cybersecurity governance

Governments also use international law in their cybersecurity governance efforts. States adopt and implement rules of international law primarily through:

- Treaties – formal, written agreements that create binding obligations for the states that enter into such agreements; and
- Customary international law – unwritten rules that reflect general and consistent state practice that states believe bind them in their international relations.

States deal with cybersecurity threats by using treaties concluded before the internet emerged, such as the UN Charter, and by adopting treaties on cybersecurity problems, such as cybercrime. Generally, states often apply pre-internet treaties because they have not, to date, adopted much treaty law that specifically addresses cybersecurity problems. States have most actively adopted new treaty law against cybercrime, but none of the

---

[9]   Mark A. Lemley, 'The Splinternet', *Duke Law Journal* 70 (2021): 1397–1427, 1399.

cybercrime treaties has garnered sufficient support from enough states to constitute a global regime for a global threat.

This situation helps explain why states have encountered difficulties agreeing on how international law applies in cyberspace. Several states have claimed that some pre-cyber treaties, such as those containing the law of armed conflict, are inadequate or inappropriate to apply in cyberspace. Other disputes about treaty law and cyber issues have arisen because states have bickered for decades, well before the internet emerged, about what treaty rules mean, such as the prohibition on the use of force. The sparsity of agreements specifically addressing cybersecurity problems indicates that states have shown little interest in, or the ability to agree on, treaty-based strategies and rules. The failure of ITU members to reach consensus on revising one of its treaties, the ITRs, because of disagreements about cybersecurity illustrates this pattern.

A similar dynamic exists with customary international law. Typically, customary international law develops over time as state practice gradually converges into patterns of behaviour that states believe become binding rules of international law. Cybersecurity is a relatively new problem, having emerged as the internet developed into a global resource since the mid-1990s. As noted above, internet and cybersecurity governance in this period did not follow the traditional pattern of intergovernmental cooperation and international legal agreements that characterized how states had previously managed the cross-border aspects of ICTs. Controversies between the multi-stakeholder and intergovernmental approaches to internet governance, the proliferation of cybersecurity problems among states, and divergent government responses to cybersecurity threats make it difficult to identify general and consistent patterns of state behaviour that countries believe have coalesced into rules of customary international law.

Problems with applying pre-cyber treaties and customary international law also appear because countries have been reluctant to make their positions on cyber incidents and issues clear, which limits the state practice that lawyers can analyse in interpreting treaties or applying customary international law. This problem has stimulated efforts by international lawyers to issue documents on how international law applies to cyber activities.[10] In recent years, several countries have issued statements containing their views on the application of international law in cyberspace. Although welcome as additional evidence that countries agree that international law applies in cyberspace, these statements often remain general and are not necessarily helpful in analysing whether specific cyber incidents violated international law.

More broadly, states often take positions on international law concerning cyber issues that appear inconsistent. As seen in the revision of the ITRs and the initiation of UN negotiations on a new cybercrime convention (Section 3.3), China and Russia have led efforts to revise or create treaty law on internet governance and cybersecurity. However, the Chinese and Russian hard-line positions on internet sovereignty create problems for the application of existing bodies of treaty law, such as international human rights law. The United States has opposed attempts to subject internet governance to international law and efforts to revise existing agreements or create new treaties to address cybersecurity issues. But the United States interprets international law on sovereignty and non-intervention to accommodate internet freedom and insists that pre-existing bodies of international law, such as on human rights and armed conflict, apply in cyberspace.

Sceptics would interpret Chinese, Russian, and US behaviour as cyber examples of the long-standing habit of great powers to treat international law like a buffet – selecting only the portions that serve their respective power and interests. Under this perspective, cybersecurity does not escape the power politics that affects international law in all other policy areas. Such *realpolitik* creates obstacles for intergovernmental, multi-stakeholder, and non-governmental efforts to clarify how international law applies in cyberspace. It blocks adoption of new international law on cybersecurity problems. It also stymies the potential for non-binding norms of responsible state behaviour in cyberspace to become codified in treaty law or recognized as customary international

---

[10]   See, e.g., the NATO Cooperative Cyber Defence Centre of Excellence's support of the production of manuals on the application of international law to cyber operations and the Oxford Process on International Law Protections in Cyberspace, sponsored by the University of Oxford and Microsoft, that has issued statements on how international law applies to different cyber threats.

law. The return of balance-of-power politics to the international system, and the drawing of geopolitical boundaries across cyberspace, mean that rival great powers will likely take positions that undermine prospects for international law to have an expanded and more effective role in cybersecurity over the next decade.

PART II

Cybersecurity and non-state actors:
Crime and terrorism in cyberspace

3 Cybercrime

The scale, intensity, and diversity of cybercrime have reached such proportions that many countries consider it a national security threat. The magnitude of the problem creates hard questions because cybercrime has been the cybersecurity issue on which states have developed the most domestic and international law. This chapter introduces the cybercrime problem (Section 3.1), analyses how governments use domestic criminal law against it (Section 3.2), and examines the ways states apply international law to counter cybercrime (Section 3.3). It considers cybercrime under both prongs of this book's definition of cybersecurity – defending against cybercrime, and law-enforcement use of cyber technologies to investigate criminal activity. Given the severity of the cybercrime challenge, the chapter also considers alternative approaches focused on strengthening cyber defences and creating cyber deterrence (Sections 3.2.5 and 3.3.4).

The chapter does not address all criminal activity relevant to cybersecurity. Cyber terrorism and cyber espionage implicate criminal law (Chapters 4 and 5). Domestic and international law contain rules prohibiting war crimes that use of cyber weapons in armed conflict could violate (Chapter 6). This chapter also does not explore all crimes committed online, such as distribution of child pornography. Many of these crimes do not involve unauthorized access to, and manipulation of, cyber technologies and are not cybersecurity issues.

3.1   The cybercrime problem

Criminals always exploit new ICTs. The telegraph, telephone, radio, and television expanded opportunities for criminals to defraud people. In response, governments criminalized 'wire fraud'. The spread of computers into businesses and homes in the 1980s gave criminals new tools and targets, which produced laws on 'computer crimes', such as the US Computer Fraud and Abuse Act (1984). The internet provided criminals with more ways to commit wire fraud and computer crimes but on a scale, intensity, and sophistication beyond anything previously experienced in criminal exploitation of ICTs. Governments turned to criminal law to combat 'cybercrime' (Section 3.2).

Unfortunately, descriptions of the cybercrime problem make grim reading. Cybercrime imposes enormous costs globally, is lucrative for transnational criminal organizations, consumes more and more law-enforcement resources, and is expanding around the world. The European Law Enforcement Agency (Europol) asserted in 2016 that cybercrime's 'volume, scope and financial damage … has reached such a level that in some EU countries cybercrime may have surpassed traditional crime in terms of reporting'.[1] In 2018, James Lewis, a leading cybersecurity expert, argued that cybercrime had become 'relentless, undiminished, and unlikely to stop'.[2] In its *Internet Organised Crime Threat Assessment* (2020), Europol stressed how cybercriminals expand their activities by using new methods (e.g., ransomware), developing new technologies (e.g., cryptocurrencies), and exploiting socio-economic conditions, such as how the COVID-19 pandemic increased cyber vulnerabilities by forcing businesses and individuals to depend even more on internet communications.

Cybercrime is a complex phenomenon, but a fertile technological context, a difficult legal environment, and contentious political dynamics combine to drive its exponential growth. Internet-linked technologies provide criminals with powerful capabilities and expanding opportunities. Innovation enhances these capabilities, such as through encryption software that frustrates law-enforcement investigations (Section 3.2.4). Innovation also generates more opportunities, such as the cybercrime bonanza the 'internet of things' produces. Increasingly, law-enforcement agencies find that all criminal activity involves some cyber component.

---

[1]   European Law Enforcement Agency, *Internet Organised Crime Threat Assessment 2016*, 7.

[2]   James A. Lewis, *Economic Impact of Cybercrime – No Slowing Down* (Center for Strategic and International Studies and McAfee, 2018), 3.

However, domestic and international legal rules do not function as interoperable protocols in an open-architecture network. Borders matter in how law works, so states must align domestic laws through intergovernmental mechanisms, such as treaties, to bring cybercriminals to justice (Section 3.3). Political disagreements among states produce contentious, fragmented cooperation. The return of geopolitics in international relations makes achieving cooperation more difficult. Put simply, technology provides cybercriminals with efficient means to operate within and across countries, while law and politics force governments to use inefficient approaches that generate ineffective outcomes at home and abroad.

Cybercrime's growth has renewed commitment to traditional strategies and sparked interest in new ideas to fight cybercrime (Section 3.2.5). Several alternative approaches tackle the problem without relying on criminal law. For example, regulatory mandates and tort law are tools that could support better private-sector cyber defences against cybercrime. Debates have emerged about whether to allow corporations to 'hack back' against cybercriminals to achieve cyber deterrence. Governments are exploring how to use international law to require states to act against cybercrime activities in their territories that cause harm in other countries, and, if this obligation is violated, whether governments can launch offensive cyber operations against foreign criminal groups to stop and deter cybercrime (Section 3.3.4).

3.2   Cybercrime and domestic law

In fighting cybercrime, governments have used two strategies. First, governments apply general criminal law, including the crimes of identity theft, wire fraud, and infringement of intellectual property rights. Second, governments have created new offences prohibiting activities specifically associated with cybercrime, such as gaining unauthorized access to a computer, as well as new rules of criminal procedure, such as expedited preservation of digital evidence. In 2020, the UN Commission on Trade and Development reported that 154 countries, or approximately 80 per cent of UN members, have adopted cybercrime legislation. Law-enforcement agencies often use general criminal law and specific cybercrime law in investigating and prosecuting cybercriminals. This section focuses on the domestic criminal law states have adopted to combat cybercrime.

3.2.1   Jurisdictional issues

Domestic cybercrime laws raise jurisdictional issues.[3] Given cybercrime's global range, whether domestic law on cybercrime applies extraterritorially is important. International law permits states to prescribe domestic law to activities outside their respective territories when those activities are undertaken by nationals or have significant effects within a state (Section 3.3.1). National legal systems also have rules that determine whether domestic laws apply extraterritorially. For example, US federal laws do not apply extraterritorially unless Congress made it clear in enacting the laws that they have extraterritorial application.

Domestic cybercrime law would not be effective if it only applied to activities happening inside a country's borders. This need for extraterritorial reach explains why model domestic cybercrime laws developed by regional organizations (Sections 3.2.2 and 3.2.3) include provisions to ensure that a government at least establishes jurisdiction over offences committed outside its territory by one of its nationals or on a ship or aircraft registered under national law. Countries also often extend criminal jurisdiction over offences committed abroad by foreign nationals that are intended to have, or have, effects within their sovereign territory. For example, South African courts have criminal jurisdiction over acts constituting cybercrime offences 'where any result of the offence has had an effect in the Republic' and acts that affect, or are intended to affect 'a public body, a business, or any other person in the Republic' (Cybercrimes and Cybersecurity Bill, B6-2017, secs. 23(1)(b) and 23(3)(a)). More difficult extraterritorial problems arise when governments want to obtain evidence or gain custody of suspects located in other countries (Section 3.3.2).

Jurisdictional issues also appear in countries with federal systems of government where both central and sub-national governments can adopt cybercrime laws. However, the way the internet links ICTs across borders, both within a country and between nations, usually triggers the criminal jurisdiction of central governments. Such governments might not exer-

---

[3]   On jurisdiction and cyberspace generally, see Uta Kohl, 'Jurisdiction in Network Society', in Nicholas Tsagourias and Russell Buchan, eds, *Research Handbook on International Law and Cyberspace* (Edward Elgar, 2nd edn, 2021) [hereinafter *Research Handbook on International Law and Cyberspace*], 69–96.

cise jurisdiction in every case, but the blurred boundaries of cyberspace make it difficult to deny that, as a matter of domestic law in federal states, the central government has jurisdiction over most cybercrime within its territory or, if initiated from abroad, affecting persons or activities in its territory.

The global scope of cybercrime creates jurisdictional issues when countries investigating cybercrimes need evidence or custody over suspected perpetrators found in other states. International law does not permit a state to exercise enforcement jurisdiction, such as conducting criminal investigations, within another state without its permission (Section 3.3.1). This prohibition forces countries to develop agreements that facilitate extradition of criminal suspects and cooperation on criminal investigations (Sections 3.3.2 and 3.3.3).

3.2.2   Substantive criminal law

Countries have responded to cybercrime by criminalizing behaviour that makes ICTs the subject (or target) and the instrument (or means) of crimes. An ICT device or system is the subject of a crime when, for example, someone gains unauthorized access to it. A device or system is the instrument of a crime when a person uses it to commit crimes, such as identity theft or distribution of child pornography. For cybersecurity, the crimes of concern are those in which ICT devices and systems are both the subject and the instrument of the crime, as happens, for example, in using a computer to hack into another computer to plant malware.

Cybercrime laws often define 'computers', 'computer systems', or 'information systems' broadly given the diversity of ICTs. For example, the Southern African Development Community's model domestic cybercrime law from 2013 defines a 'computer system' as 'a device or a group of inter-connected or related devices, one or more of which, pursuant to a program, performs automatic processing of data or other functions' (art. 3(5)). In creating specific offences, cybercrime laws sometimes define more specific categories, such as computers used by financial institutions or government agencies.

Cybercrime laws generally prohibit, and authorize punishment of, certain actions involving cyber technologies. Most often, these offences criminalize intentional acts involving unauthorized:

- Access to, use of, or interference with computing devices and systems;
- Access to, use of, interference with, theft of, or damage to data located on computing devices and systems;
- Interception of data transmitted between computing devices and systems; and
- Production, possession, acquisition, or use of items (e.g., software) with the intent to commit a criminal offence concerning computing devices, systems, and data.[4]

As with other domestic criminal legislation, cybercrime laws contain the elements of the offences, including the mental state (*mens rea*) required, and provide punishments (e.g., fines, imprisonment). The elements of the offences often include terms or concepts that have specific definitions to ensure clarity in the law's application.

Domestic cybercrime laws differ because some governments include offences other countries do not criminalize. This divergence is most apparent with the content of online communications. Most countries criminalize online child pornography, but criminal codes and model cybercrime laws often include content-based offences that criminalize online harassment, defamation, hate speech, religious acts (e.g., blasphemy), and all forms of pornography.[5] Authoritarian governments frequently criminalize online speech that threatens social order and their power. Such content-based offences fall outside the realm of cybersecurity as defined in this book, but they raise policy and legal questions concerning, for example, freedom of expression.

---

[4]   Model domestic cybercrime laws contain these core offences. See, e.g., Commonwealth Model Law on Computer and Computer-Related Crime (2002), arts 5–9.

[5]   See, e.g., Pacific Island Regional Model Cybercrime Legislation (2013), arts 12, 17, 20, and 21.

3.2.3   Criminal procedure and law-enforcement access to electronic data and communications

In adopting cybercrime laws, governments must think about criminal procedure. To investigate cybercrimes, law-enforcement agencies need access to stored and real-time electronic communications, metadata about such communications, and content. For some governments, general powers to conduct law-enforcement investigations, such as powers to conduct searches and seizures, provide sufficient authority for investigating cybercrimes. Other governments have adopted new laws to ensure cybercrime investigations can access pertinent electronic communications and data.

Model domestic cybercrime laws include provisions on criminal procedure to encourage governments to assess whether their laws are sufficient and guide governments that decide to revise their laws. For example, the Commonwealth Model Law on Computer and Computer-Related Crime (2002) contains articles on search-and-seizure warrants; assisting police investigations; providing records of and access to seized data; production of data; disclosure of stored traffic data; preservation of data; interception of electronic communications; interception of traffic data; admission of evidence; confidentiality of lawful orders; and limitation of liability for lawful disclosures (arts 11–21).

ICT innovations, such as mobile telephony and internet-enabled digital communications, have forced governments to make sure law-enforcement agencies can access new types of electronic data and communications in criminal investigations. Some laws impose requirements on communication-service providers to configure services and software to maintain technical access for implementation of lawful orders, such as search-and-seizure warrants.[6] The ability of criminals to move geographically and use different technologies created challenges for legal powers that historically applied to searches and seizures at specific places. Governments need to decide when 'roving wiretaps' or 'roving interceptions' should be permissible. New, undisclosed software vulnerabilities – known as 'zero-day vulnerabilities' – also create opportunities for law-enforcement agencies to conduct searches and seizures

---

6   See, e.g., the US Communications Assistance for Law Enforcement Act 1994.

through 'lawful hacking', a technique that has raised legal and policy questions.[7] In the context of a global internet, domestic law does not give law-enforcement agencies authority to obtain evidence of alleged crimes located within other states. Criminal use of cyber technologies has revealed problems with traditional strategies for international law-enforcement cooperation, and responses to these problems have implications for domestic laws on law-enforcement access to electronic communications and data (Section 3.3.2).

The need to adapt law to ensure law-enforcement access to electronic data and communications for criminal investigations in the wake of technological innovation created controversies centred on privacy rights in constitutional and statutory law. The challenge for domestic law remains the same – balancing law-enforcement needs for access to information in investigating crime and protecting the individual's right to privacy. On this question, countries strike different balances between law-enforcement powers and individual privacy.

Divergence is apparent when comparing not only democratic and authoritarian countries but also democracies. The United States and the EU share a common approach to cybercrime (Section 3.3.3), but US and EU privacy laws differ, which creates tension in the transatlantic movement of digital information for law enforcement and commercial purposes.[8] Model domestic cybercrime laws also exhibit variation, with the model law developed for the Caribbean criticized for supporting 'unbridled powers without … civil liberty protections necessary with respect to criminal investigation and prosecution'.[9]

3.2.4   Law enforcement, encryption, and 'going dark'

In response to efforts to maintain and expand law-enforcement authority to access electronic data and communications, cybercriminals and privacy advocates have embraced, for different reasons, encryption to

---

[7]   See discussion of the controversy concerning whether governments disclose zero-day vulnerabilities or keep them secret for law enforcement, intelligence, or military purposes in Section 5.3.3.

[8]   On EU law and cyberspace generally, see Ramses A. Wessel, 'European Law and Cyberspace', in *Research Handbook on International Law and Cyberspace*, 490–507.

[9]   Zahid Jamil, *Cybercrime Model Laws* (Council of Europe, 2014), 11–12.

protect information and communications. Cybersecurity experts support increased use of encryption to strengthen cyber defences. However, encrypted data and communications alarm law-enforcement agencies because encryption threatens their ability to investigate criminal activity.[10] Law-enforcement officials around the world have argued that cyberspace is 'going dark' because criminal use of encryption is proliferating.

The going-dark problem has stimulated efforts, proposals, and laws focused on providing governments with the ability to bypass encryption by, for example, exploiting 'back doors' built into encryption software. Australia's Telecommunications and Other Legislation Amendment (Assistance and Access) Act (2018) gave the government the authority to require communication-service companies to ensure that they can provide communications to the government in connection with criminal and national security investigations. China legally requires 'tech companies to provide technical and decryption assistance for public security and intelligence gathering purposes'.[11] By contrast, no federal legislation has been adopted in the United States because consensus on how to handle the going-dark problem has not emerged despite law-enforcement officials warning about the threat that encryption poses. This stalemate reflects how cybersecurity experts and privacy advocates emphasize encryption's benefits, the dangers 'back doors' in encryption software would create, and the availability of other strategies law-enforcement agencies can use to address the encryption challenge, such as lawful hacking.

Debates about the challenges that encryption poses to law enforcement have been national in scope. However, cybercrime – and many other criminal activities that exploit the internet – is global in scope. Legal requirements for communication companies in Australia to provide the Australian government with unencrypted data have no legal effect on transnational criminal organizations that deploy encryption software developed and used outside Australia. Unlike international harmonization of cybercrime laws (Section 3.3.3), no equivalent attempt to harmonize national law-enforcement approaches to encryption has materialized.

---

[10]   Encryption also raises concerns for counterterrorism (Section 4.4.1) and counterintelligence (Section 5.3.2).

[11]   Lorand Laski and Adam Segal, *The Encryption Debate in China* (Carnegie Endowment for International Peace, 2019).

3.2.5 'Harden the target' and 'hacking back': Cyber defence and cyber deterrence

The emphasis on encryption to strengthen cyber defences highlights a broader problem. Clearly, domestic criminal laws do not deter cyber-criminals around the world. These laws do not produce 'deterrence by norms', and the threat of legal sanctions does not generate 'deterrence by punishment'. The effectiveness of categorizing a cyber threat as a crime is suspect, which informs interest in alternative strategies. Using criminal law largely involves reacting to cybersecurity harms rather than preventing and protecting against cybercrime. Seeking prevention and protection moves policy away from slotting cybersecurity incidents into traditional national security categories, such as crime, and towards cyber-defence and cyber-deterrence strategies. Achieving better prevention of, and protection against, cybercrime requires exploring strategies that do not depend on criminal law.

One alternative approach seeks to 'harden the target' by improving cyber defences against crime and other cyber threats. Although cybercrime has increased for years, companies continue to underinvest in cyber defence. Strategies that seek to increase incentives for companies to strengthen cyber defences include:

- Applying non-cyber regulatory regimes, such as laws prohibiting unfair and deceptive trade practices or requiring information disclosure to shareholders, that force companies to be transparent about their cybersecurity policies, practices, and incidents;
- Mandating that private-sector enterprises improve their cyber defences in accordance with specified cybersecurity standards and best practices;[12]
- Deploying tort law and litigation by individuals affected by cyber-crime to encourage companies to improve software and corporate cybersecurity;
- Using cybersecurity insurance to promote stronger cybersecurity practices by the private sector in return for better coverage and lower premiums; and

---

[12]   This strategy also appears in protecting critical infrastructure against cyber terrorism (Section 4.3.1).

- Bolstering cyber defences through preventive and protective measures modelled on public health and environmental protection strategies.

None of these strategies has gained sufficient traction to be identified as the leading candidate for strengthening domestic cyber defences against cybercrime. In some countries, government regulation might be better because tort law and insurance markets are less developed. In other countries, political interests might prefer to let markets sort things out rather than impose legal mandates. Domestic laws on public health and environmental protection vary, and much evidence suggests they are not effective in many countries. The COVID-19 pandemic has been a calamity despite decades of emphasis on pandemic preparedness, which undercuts public health's credibility as a model for cybersecurity. Similarly, the climate change crisis demonstrates that environmental laws have failed in most countries to mitigate greenhouse gas emissions or prepare societies to adapt to the problems that climate change creates.

A second approach focuses on allowing private-sector enterprises to engage in so-called 'active defence' against cybercrime. Active defence has no agreed meaning, but, typically, it encompasses 'trace back' and 'hack back' actions. In short, the approach would allow companies to go beyond passive defence (e.g., intrusion detection) to retaliate against cybercriminals by reaching into their systems to gather evidence of illegal activity (trace back) or manipulate those systems to damage them or recover stolen digital property (hack back). The rationale is to create deterrence against cybercrime through private-sector offensive cyber measures. This perspective holds that achieving better cyber defences (deterrence by denial) is not sufficient and that empowering the private sector to retaliate (deterrence by punishment) is needed. Here, the shift in policy interest towards the cyber-deterrence approach is apparent in the cybercrime context.

However, the active-defence strategy is fraught with problems. For critics, private-sector active defence enables cyber vigilantism, which will make cyberspace more insecure. Many corporate victims of cybercrime do not have the capability to hack back. Cybercriminals might not be deterred and might escalate through more cybercrime or physical violence against company property or personnel.

The active-defence strategy also creates legal concerns. Under most domestic cybercrime laws, active-defence measures would violate the law of the country where the measures originated and where the target is located. Revising national law to allow active-defence actions would not make such actions legal in the jurisdiction where the target is found. Government authorization of active defence by private-sector actors, or governmental action to 'hack back' on behalf of companies, would violate both customary international law on enforcement jurisdiction (Section 3.3.1) and treaties on law-enforcement cooperation and cybercrime (Sections 3.3.2 and 3.3.3).

3.3   Cybercrime and international law

Cybercrime's global nature, combined with how international law structures jurisdiction, has led countries to use international law in combating cybercrime.[13] This section describes how international law affects the exercise of criminal jurisdiction (Section 3.3.1) and forces states to cooperate on law enforcement through extradition and mutual legal assistance treaties (Section 3.3.2). States used this approach in adopting treaties on cybercrime (Section 3.3.3). States have not used international law much to advance cyber defences against cybercrime. In response to cybercrime incidents involving critical infrastructure, countries have turned to international law to emphasize the obligation for governments to mitigate the transboundary harm that cybercrime creates and, if governments refuse to mitigate, to justify offensive cyber operations against foreign cybercriminals (Section 3.3.4).

3.3.1   Sovereignty, non-intervention, and jurisdiction to prescribe and enforce law

International law permits states to exercise 'prescriptive jurisdiction' over certain activities taking place outside their territories but prohibits states from exercising 'enforcement jurisdiction' within other states without consent. As Section 3.2.1 noted, a country can prescribe cybercrime laws for extraterritorial activities undertaken by (1) its nationals (the nationality principle); or (2) foreign nationals whose actions outside its

---

[13]   See, e.g., Philipp Kastner and Frédéric Mégret, 'International Legal Dimensions of Cybercrime', in *Research Handbook on International Law and Cyberspace*, 252–69.

territory have substantial effects within its territory (the effects principle).[14] However, the state cannot engage in law-enforcement activities, such as conducting criminal investigations, inside another state without its permission.

The rules on prescriptive and enforcement jurisdiction flow from international legal doctrine on sovereignty and non-intervention. In international law, sovereignty means that a state has supreme authority over its territory. Thus, states must respect the sovereignty of other states. The power to enforce criminal law is fundamental to sovereign authority because it constitutes an exercise of the state's coercive power within its territory. The non-intervention rule supplements sovereignty by prohibiting a state from intervening in the domestic affairs of other states.

The sovereignty and non-intervention rules have created controversies, including in connection with state behaviour in cyberspace;[15] but all countries agree that a state's attempt to enforce its criminal law within the territory of another state without consent would violate these rules. Extraterritorial prescription of criminal law does not violate the sovereignty and non-intervention rules because (1) states share a common interest in exercising prescriptive jurisdiction in permitted circumstances, including applying the nationality and effects principles; and (2) states cooperate on law-enforcement matters, such as gaining custody over alleged perpetrators located in other countries, associated with the exercise of extraterritorial prescription of criminal law.

3.3.2 Extradition and mutual legal assistance treaties

Given international law on sovereignty, non-intervention, and enforcement jurisdiction, states must cooperate on cross-border law-enforcement

---

[14] International law permits the exercise of prescriptive jurisdiction extraterritorially on other grounds, such as to protect a state's vital interests – the protective principle. Concerning cybercrime, the nationality and the effects principles are the most important. For more, see American Law Institute, *Restatement (Fourth) of the Foreign Relations Law of the United States* (2018), secs 408–13 (prescriptive jurisdiction) and 432 (enforcement jurisdiction).

[15] On these controversies, see Chapters 5 (cyber espionage) and 6 (cyber war).

activities.[16] States have used bilateral treaties on extradition and mutual legal assistance to operationalize such cooperation. Extradition involves the surrender of a person by a state to another state for criminal prosecution or punishment, and extradition treaties regulate this process. Mutual legal assistance treaties (MLATs) obligate states parties to cooperate on law-enforcement matters, such as collecting evidence in criminal investigations.

Even though some states have negotiated cybercrime treaties (Section 3.3.3), understanding how extradition treaties and MLATs function remains important for law-enforcement approaches to cybercrime. Cybercrime treaties contain provisions on extradition and mutual legal assistance modelled on what states have done in bilateral treaties on these issues. In addition, not all states have joined the same cybercrime treaties, so states often use bilateral extradition agreements and MLATs in cooperating on cybercrime.

Turning first to extradition, countries can extradite individuals without a treaty, but treaties have become the standard mechanism for this type of law-enforcement cooperation. Most countries have signed several bilateral extradition treaties, which contain common approaches refined over decades. The UN Model Treaty on Extradition (1990) reflects these approaches and informs the following description of bilateral extradition treaties.

Parties to extradition treaties agree to extradite any person located in the requested state and wanted in the requesting state for prosecution of, or imposition of a sentence related to, an extraditable offence. Extradition treaties apply to criminal activities generally, so extraditable offences cover a range of crimes that impose sentences of a specified duration, such as imprisonment for a least one year. Extraditable offences must be criminal offences under the laws of both parties (the double criminality principle). Law-enforcement agencies use extradition treaties to obtain

---

[16]   States recognized the need for cooperation in creating the International Criminal Police Organization (INTERPOL). INTERPOL facilitates the sharing of information among the law-enforcement agencies of its members, and it provides members technical and operational support. Among many other criminal challenges, INTERPOL helps its members cooperate on cybercrime.

custody over persons alleged to have committed cybercrime offences, which illustrates the utility of the broad scope that such treaties have.

Extradition treaties provide the requested state with mandatory and optional grounds for refusing to extradite a person. Mandatory grounds justify refusing requests based on, for example, political offences, such as charging a person with a crime for engaging in peaceful civil disobedience, or if an extradited person would be tortured. States parties to extradition treaties can use optional grounds for refusing extradition requests if, for example, the offence triggers capital punishment in the requesting state or if the person subject to an extradition request is a national of the requested state. Extradition treaties prohibit the requesting state from prosecuting an extradited person for crimes other than the offences used for the extradition unless the requested state consents (the speciality principle). The treaties contain procedural provisions that address, among other things, how states parties communicate concerning extradition requests. Within this structure, countries negotiate specific rules for their bilateral law-enforcement cooperation. For example, some extradition treaties declare that terrorist offences are not political offences and do not permit using the political-offence doctrine to refuse an extradition request for such offences.

For other types of law-enforcement cooperation, bilateral MLATs provide the substantive and procedural rules that guide how countries provide legal assistance in criminal matters. Countries typically have many MLATs, which usually apply to a broad range of issues, including assistance in taking statements of persons, providing documents for evidence, and executing requests for searches and seizures. The treaties prescribe the form, content, and specific requirements for legal assistance requests and require a central authority in each state party to make and receive such requests. MLATs have rules that allow a requested state to deny assistance, such as when a request for assistance would prejudice national security.

Countries use MLATs in investigating cybercrimes that have international features. However, the transnational nature of cybercrime has produced concerns that MLATs are inadequate. For many governments, the MLAT process is too slow and cumbersome to be effective in the cyber age. Interest has emerged in reforming MLATs or developing new strategies on cybercrime and other crimes that involve exploiting the internet.

The United States and the United Kingdom (UK) agreed to allow their respective law-enforcement agencies to seek information directly from companies located in the other country, rather than routing requests for legal assistance through government bodies. The United States adopted the Clarifying Lawful Overseas Use of Data (CLOUD) Act (2018) to make this approach possible, and the United States and the UK entered into the Agreement on Access to Electronic Data for the Purpose of Countering Serious Crime (2019) to implement the strategy. The US-UK agreement broke new ground, and the United States is negotiating similar agreements with Australia and the EU. But, until more countries follow suit, MLATs remain the dominant mechanism for mutual legal assistance on cybercrime.

Table 3.1   Cybercrime treaties

International Organization	Year	Treaty
Council of Europe	2001	Convention on Cybercrime
Commonwealth of Independent States	2001	Agreement on Cooperation in Combating Offenses Related to Computer Information
Shanghai Cooperation Organization	2009	Agreement on Cooperation in the Field of International Information Security
League of Arab States	2010	Arab Convention on Combating Information Technology Offenses
African Union	2014	African Convention on Cyber Security and Personal Data Protection

3.3.3   Harmonizing domestic law and facilitating law-enforcement cooperation through cybercrime treaties

In addition to extradition treaties and MLATs, states have negotiated agreements to facilitate law-enforcement action and cooperation in specific areas of criminal law, such as terrorism (Chapter 4). Countries have concluded new treaties specifically to address cybercrime (Table 3.1) and have discussed the applicability of the UN Convention on Transnational Organized Crime (2000) to cybercrime. UN discussions for a comprehensive cybercrime treaty are also underway (UN Doc. A/RES/74/247 (2019)).

The negotiation of cybercrime treaties reflects the seriousness of the cybercrime problem, but the different treaties reflect the inability of states to agree on a common approach. The leading treaty is the Convention on Cybercrime created by the Council of Europe (COE). As of October 2021, the Convention had 66 states parties, including the United States and leading European countries, such as France, Germany, and the UK. However, only about one-third of UN member states have joined the COE convention. Important countries, such as China and Russia, oppose it, have created alternatives (e.g., the Shanghai Cooperation Organization's agreement), and support the UN process for developing a comprehensive treaty on criminal use of ICTs. The League of Arab States and the African Union developed treaties rather than encouraging their members to join the COE convention, but acceptance of these treaties is not impressive. Only eight of the 55 members of the African Union had ratified the African convention as of June 2020.

The number and diversity of treaties addressing cybercrime counsels caution in analysing them for common characteristics. Generally, the treaties require states to (1) take jurisdiction over the crimes covered; (2) harmonize domestic law on cybercrime offences and criminal procedure; and (3) establish mechanisms for law-enforcement cooperation, such as extradition and mutual legal assistance. Table 3.2 provides examples of treaty provisions on these issues.

The jurisdiction and harmonization strategies ensure that states parties have equivalent legal approaches to cybercrime. Having the same jurisdictional reach and criminal offences across countries plugs gaps that cybercriminals exploit and facilitates law-enforcement assistance because, for example, having common offences means the principle of double criminality used in extradition is satisfied. Although the treaties share these features, they differ in the criminal offences and procedural law harmonized and the law-enforcement assistance established.

As with model domestic cybercrime laws (Section 3.2.2), cybercrime treaties contain different substantive criminal offences. The treaties include offences that fall within the definition of cybersecurity used in this book, such as illicit access to computer systems and illegal damaging of computer data. The treaties also include criminal offences that are not cybersecurity threats, which typically are content-based offences, such as child pornography, or crimes facilitated through ICTs, such as human trafficking.

Table 3.2   Examples of provisions in cybercrime treaties

Jurisdiction

Council of Europe, Convention on Cybercrime
Article 22 – Jurisdiction

1. Each Party shall adopt such legislative and other measures as may be necessary to establish jurisdiction over any offence established in accordance with Articles 2 through 11 of this Convention, when the offence is committed:

   a. in its territory; or
   b. on board a ship flying the flag of that Party; or
   c. on board an aircraft registered under the laws of that Party; or
   d. by one of its nationals, if the offence is punishable under criminal law where it was committed or if the offence is committed outside the territorial jurisdiction of any State ...

Harmonization of Criminal Offences

League of Arab States, Arab Convention on Combating Information Technology Offenses
Article 5: Criminalization
Every State Party shall commit itself to the criminalization of acts set forth in this chapter, according to its legislations and statutes.

Article 6: Offense of Illicit Access

1. Illicit access to, presence in or contact with part or all of the information technology, or the perpetuation thereof.
2. The punishment shall be increased if this access, presence, contact or perpetuation leads to:

   a. the obliteration, modification, distortion, duplication, removal or destruction of saved data, electronic instruments and systems and communication networks, and damages to the users and beneficiaries.
   b. the acquirement of secret government information ...

Harmonization of Procedural Law

African Union, African Convention on Cyber Security and Personal Data Protection
Article 31 – Adapting Certain Sanctions to Information and Communication Technologies

3. Procedural law

   a. States Parties shall take the necessary legislative measures to ensure that where the data stored in a computer system or in a medium where computerized data can be stored in the territory of a State Party, are useful in establishing the truth, the court applied to may carry out a search to access all or part of a computer system through another computer system, where the said data are accessible from or available to the initial system ....

Establishment of Mechanisms for Law Enforcement Assistance

Council of Europe, Convention on Cybercrime
Article 24 – Extradition

1.
   a. This article applies to extradition between Parties for the criminal offences established in accordance with Articles 2 through 11 of this Convention, provided that they are punishable under the laws of both Parties concerned by deprivation of liberty for a maximum period of at least one year, or by a more severe penalty ...

2. The criminal offences described in paragraph 1 of this article shall be deemed to be included as extraditable offences in any extradition treaty existing between or among the Parties. The Parties undertake to include such offences as extraditable offences in any extradition treaty to be concluded between or among them.

3. If a Party that makes extradition conditional on the existence of a treaty receives a request for extradition from another Party with which it does not have an extradition treaty, it may consider this Convention as the legal basis for extradition with respect to any criminal offence referred to in paragraph 1 of this article ...

Variation appears as well across the treaties on mechanisms of law-enforcement cooperation. The treaties typically include provisions for extradition and mutual legal assistance, but they can differ on how they deal with these processes. Under the COE convention (art. 24(3)) and the Arab League convention (art. 31(3)), if two states parties do not have a bilateral extradition treaty, they can use the respective convention as the legal instrument facilitating extradition. By contrast, the African convention does not have such a provision, meaning states parties need to use extradition treaties for the crimes it covers.

Harmonization of procedural law is also an area where states have taken different positions. China and Russia have opposed the COE convention on sovereignty grounds concerning its article 32, which allows a state party to obtain computer data in the territory of another state party without that party's authorization. Although states parties to the COE convention disagree with the Chinese and Russian interpretation of this provision, the issue remains one of the reasons why many countries have not joined the convention.

These differences across cybercrime treaties on substantive offences, procedural law, and law-enforcement assistance suggest that UN negotiations on a comprehensive treaty on criminal use of ICTs will experience difficulties. The COE convention's history indicates that states 'disagree about what digital practices should be outlawed and are deeply skeptical about even the weakest forms of international cooperation in this area', which serves as 'a cautionary tale for those who believe in the feasibility of a broader cybersecurity treaty'.[17] Nothing has happened since the COE convention's adoption concerning divergent policy and legal approaches to cybercrime that would indicate disagreements about the convention have dissipated. Any treaty produced by the UN negotiations will likely be accepted only by some countries, an outcome that will contribute to the fragmentation already evident with cybercrime treaties.

Finally, whether cybercrime treaties contribute much to the fight against cybercrime is doubtful. The COE convention entered into force in 2004 and has the most states parties among the cybercrime treaties, but cybercrime has only increased since its adoption. In 2016, the Europol director argued that '[t]he relentless growth of cybercrime remains a real and significant threat' and expressed concerns that 'an expanding cyber-criminal community' continues to 'exploit our increasing dependence on technology and the Internet'.[18] These comments about cybercrime in Europe – the COE convention's centre of gravity – provide little basis for concluding that the convention is effective.

3.3.4   International law and cybercrime: Cyber defence and cyber deterrence

Cyber defence

Interest in improving cyber defences against cybercrime has not produced much international law. Domestic cyber defence falls within a state's sovereign authority, and governments can strengthen national cyber defences without treaties or customary international law. States cooperate on cyber defence in different venues, such as the Global Forum on Cyber Expertise, by sharing information, exchanging best practices, and cooperating on capacity building. However, these activities are usually associated with voluntary cyber norms rather than binding agreements. UN efforts on cyber norms have noted that states should 'cooperate in developing and applying measures to increase stability and security in

---

17   Jack Goldsmith, *Cybersecurity Treaties: A Skeptical View* (Koret-Taube Task Force on National Security and Law, 2011), 3–4.

18   Europol, 'The Relentless Growth of Cybercrime', Press Release, 27 September 2016.

the use of ICTs' (UN Doc. A/70/174 (2015), para. 13(a)). In developing such norms, states have identified the need for governments to 'protect their critical infrastructure from ICT threats' (UN Doc. A/70/174 (2015), para. 13(g)), a context that, as discussed below, has become important in the fight against cybercrime. Cybercrime treaties that have provisions relevant to cyber defences contain broad, procedural obligations. For example, the African Convention on Cyber Security and Personal Data Protection encourages states parties to share information on cyber threats and cooperate in intergovernmental and multi-stakeholder mechanisms on improving cybersecurity (art. 28(3)–(4)).

Cyber deterrence

The increased attention cyber deterrence has received as a strategy to counter cybercrime generates international legal issues. The first context involves the interest in permitting private-sector actors to engage in active defence, such as hacking back, against cybercriminals in other countries to generate deterrence against cybercrime (Section 3.2.5). Government authorization of such active-defence actions could violate (1) applicable MLATs and cybercrime treaties, which establish rules for cooperation on cybercrime; and (2) customary international law on enforcement jurisdiction, which prohibits states from engaging in law-enforcement actions in other countries without their consent (Sections 3.3.1 and 3.3.2). The diplomatic and international legal problems that private-sector active defence would produce mean an international consensus supporting cyber deterrence as a strategy against cybercrime will not emerge.

The second context centres on frustration in many countries, especially the United States, over the perceived lack of law-enforcement action by other states against large-scale, sophisticated, and damaging cybercrime operations conducted from within those jurisdictions. Nations that have seen cybercrime against their private sectors relentlessly grow have increasingly complained that some countries, particularly China and Russia, have not cooperated on law-enforcement matters and have turned a blind eye to cybercrime that originates in their territories but focuses on foreign targets. US experts have argued that 'the "global cybercrime problem" is actually … a "Russia problem," as Putin's corrupt government and intelligence services give cover and protection to the world's largest transnational organized crimes, cybercriminals, schemes, and frauds'.[19]

These complaints have escalated with the proliferation of ransomware attacks by cybercriminals. These attacks included incidents involving US companies that operate critical infrastructure, such as health-care facilities, oil pipelines, and food production. The US government blamed cybercriminals operating from Russia for several of these attacks. The United States and Russia do not have an extradition treaty, and their MLAT has not proved helpful for US cybercrime efforts.

With traditional law-enforcement cooperation ineffective, the United States has demanded that Russia act against cybercriminal organizations in Russian territory. The United States has also threatened – and perhaps covertly conducted – offensive cyber operations against such organizations to punish the criminals and protect US critical infrastructure by deterring future attacks. In connection with the ransomware attack on an oil pipeline company, the US government announced that it had recovered the ransom by hacking the criminal group's bitcoin wallet. The threat of offensive cyber operations, the execution of covert cyber action against Russian cybercriminals, and the recovery of the bitcoin ransom raise concerns about these US actions under the international legal proscription against exercising enforcement jurisdiction in the territory of another state without its consent (Section 3.3.1). The US actions suggest that, at least concerning cybercriminals in Russia, the US government is no longer willing to rely on a law-enforcement approach.[20]

In addressing the Russian cybercrime threat, the United States has not argued that Russia ordered, or had direct control over, the ransomware attacks affecting US critical infrastructure. The US government is not using the international law of state responsibility to hold the Russian government accountable for the attacks. Nor is it claiming that Russia

---

[19]   John P. Carlin, 'The "Global Cybercrime Problem" is Actually the "Russian Problem"', *The Atlantic*, 16 December 2018.

[20]   In an October 2021 speech, the head of the UK's National Cyber Security Centre has also stated that the UK will take 'a more sustained, proactive and integrated campaign for disrupting and imposing costs on malicious actors' responsible for 'widespread criminal activity – including urgent threats such as ransomware'. National Cyber Security Centre, Lindy Cameron at Cyber 2021, Chatham House, 11 October 2021.

had violated US sovereignty or intervened in its domestic affairs. The United States has based its demands on the international legal obligation that countries exercise due diligence in not permitting territory subject to sovereign control to be used to cause harm in other states. Countries that have, or should have, knowledge of activities in their territories that cause harm in other states must act to stop them. This obligation applies in cyberspace.

This use of the due-diligence obligation in international law connects to increasing cybersecurity interest in the duty of states to act against transnational harms caused by the cyber activities of non-state actors. The *Oxford Statement on International Law Protections in Cyberspace: The Regulation of Ransomware Operations* (2021) provides that '[s]tates must not allow their territory or infrastructure under their jurisdiction or control to be used by … non-state actors for ransomware operations that are contrary to the rights of other states, when the former states know or should have known of such operations' and that 'states from which ransomware operations emanate, in full or in part, must take feasible measures to stop such operations and otherwise address the situation' (sec. 4).

In connection with the ransomware attacks on US critical infrastructure, the United States is shifting from a primary reliance on law enforcement toward the cyber-deterrence approach concerning cybercrime. The shift recalls the change in US counterterrorism policies after the 11 September 2001 terrorist attacks, when the US government moved from treating terrorism mainly as a law-enforcement problem and began using all instruments of national power, including military capabilities, against terrorism. This new posture included justifying offensive military operations against terrorist groups located in foreign countries when those countries were unable or unwilling to deal with such groups. This comparison is reflected in claims that ransomware attacks against critical infrastructure constitute terrorism.

This move generates questions under domestic and international law. The ransomware attacks causing consternation in the United States do not constitute acts of international terrorism under US law, because, for example, the groups responsible want money rather than to intimidate or coerce a civilian population or influence government policy through intimidation or coercion (Section 4.2.1). Offensive cyber operations against foreign cybercriminals are problematical under international law on enforcement jurisdiction because they seek to punish and deter criminals located in another country without its permission. Offensive cyber operations by the United States could be justified as legal countermeasures – proportionate actions otherwise illegal under international law taken in response to Russia's failure to comply with its due-diligence obligation and designed to bring Russia into compliance with that obligation.[21]

However, whether a state's non-compliance with the due-diligence obligation permits another country to exercise enforcement jurisdiction within the sovereign territory of that state under international law is doubtful. Had the United States sent federal law-enforcement agents into Russia without the Russian government's consent to investigate and arrest cybercriminals, most states would have viewed such acts as violations of international law rather than as lawful countermeasures. Given the inability of countries to agree on a definition of terrorism, attempts to categorize criminal ransomware attacks against critical infrastructure as terrorism are unlikely to gain support (Section 4.1). At present, the legal justification for offensive cyber operations against foreign cybercriminals is 'tenuous at best'.[22]

The US interest in using offensive cyber operations to punish and deter Russian cybercriminals suggests that the due-diligence obligation has had little effect against cybercrime. The US threats have not deterred Russian cybercriminals, who have continued to launch ransomware attacks on US targets while mocking claims that victims operate critical infrastructure.[23] Nor have the threats changed the behaviour of the Russian government, which has not shown much, if any, inclination to crack down on cybercriminals operating in its territory.[24]

These dynamics indicate that geopolitics, rather than international law, are driving state behaviour. China, Russia, and other countries appear

---

[21]   For discussion of countermeasures, see Michael N. Schmitt, gen. ed., *Tallinn Manual 2.0 on the International Law Applicable to Cyber Operations* (CUP, 2nd edn, 2017), 111–34.

[22]   Eric Rosenbach, Juliette Kayyem, and Lara Mitra, 'The Limits of Cyberoffense', *Foreign Affairs*, 11 August 2021.

[23]   Joseph Marks, 'Russian Hackers Deny an Iowa Grain Cooperative Counts as "Critical"', *Washington Post*, 23 September 2021.

[24]   Aaron Schaffer, 'Russian Hackers Haven't Backed Off, Administration Official Acknowledges', *Washington Post*, 6 October 2021.

willing to tolerate cybercrime operations within their territories that cause damage in the United States. The United States is threatening to escalate its responses to the cybercrime problem through offensive cyber operations to motivate its adversaries to change their behaviour.[25] Outside the realm of geopolitical rivalry, the due-diligence obligation suffers because many low-income countries do not have the capacity to act effectively against organized cybercriminal groups operating in their territories and inflicting harm in other nations.

The need perceived by the United States to threaten offensive cyber operations against foreign cybercriminals that harm the US critical infrastructure reinforces a sobering theme in this chapter – the ineffectiveness of domestic and international law on cybercrime. Unfortunately, legal, geopolitical, and technological factors continue to align in ways that promise to make cybercrime worse. The way states exercise criminal jurisdiction is so deeply rooted in how international law uses sovereignty to organize political authority that extracting efforts against most forms of cybercrime from this structure is nearly impossible. The return of balance-of-power politics makes cooperation on cybercrime harder to achieve, as the contentious UN negotiations on a comprehensive cybercrime treaty demonstrate. In the context of cybercrime affecting critical infrastructure, geopolitics are producing adversarial dynamics that could escalate cybersecurity problems among the great powers, with adverse ripple effects throughout the international system. In this environment, cybercriminals have ample opportunities and incentives to exploit innovative technologies, such as artificial intelligence, to continue to increase the scale, intensity, and sophistication of their activities around the world for years to come.

---

[25]   See also the discussion about offensive cyber operations and international law in Sections 5.4, 6.3, and 6.4.

4   Cyber terrorism

The second category of security threats that non-state actors pose is terrorism. The internet came of age when governments considered terrorism to be a growing menace. The threat extended into cyberspace, and the terrorist attacks against the United States on 11 September 2001 amplified concerns about terrorist use of the internet. This chapter describes the cyber terrorism problem (Section 4.1) and examines how governments have deployed domestic and international law to address it. In keeping with how this book defines cybersecurity, the chapter analyses how governments use law to respond to cyber terrorism (Section 4.2), defend against terrorist cyberattacks that target critical infrastructure (Section 4.3), and engage in electronic surveillance to prevent terrorism (Section 4.4). The chapter concludes by analysing how states generally use international law to combat terrorism that is relevant for cyber terrorism (Section 4.5).

4.1   The cyber terrorism problem

Terrorism has long been a controversial concept. Despite its prominence in security policy, states have never agreed on a definition of terrorism. Similar problems arise with 'cyber terrorism', which has been used to describe:

- Terrorist use of cyber weapons, operations, and attacks;
- Terrorist use of the internet for propaganda, communication, recruiting, radicalization, and fundraising; and
- Use of ICTs to engage in political speech that governments deem a threat to the state or social order.

Only the first category falls under the definition of cybersecurity used in this book. The other two involve the broader relationship between the internet, ICTs, and national security. Terrorist use of social media is a national security issue, but it is not a cybersecurity problem because the activity does not involve illicit intrusion into, manipulation of, or damage to computers, digital data, networks, or information services. This chapter primarily focuses on the domestic and international law relevant to terrorists using cyber means and methods to attack ICTs that governments and civilian populations use.[1]

Although consistent with this book's definition of cybersecurity, this approach raises questions because the world has not witnessed any widely recognized act of cyber terrorism. Instead, terrorist groups, such as the Islamic State, have exploited the internet in ways that do not involve offensive cyber operations. In addition, focusing on terrorist use of ICTs to attack governments or civilian populations does not clarify what cyber terrorism is in policy and legal terms. For example, in 2015, the Islamic State infiltrated US military computer systems and defaced web pages. The United States called the incident 'cyber vandalism' because the intrusion caused only minor, temporary disruption rather than substantial, lasting damage. Other incidents initially identified as acts of cyber terrorism – such as cyberattacks on a French television station, a German steel mill, Ukrainian electricity grids, and a German hospital – were not because investigations determined the culprits were foreign governments or cybercriminals.

The inability of states to define terrorism has not prevented governments from negotiating treaties that criminalize certain terrorist offences (Section 4.3.2). The offences in these treaties contain the common features that states use to define terrorism in policy and law. An International Law Association report identified these features in developing a definition of cyber terrorism:

> Acts intentionally committed by any person who uses information and communication technologies unlawfully in ways that cause, or are intended to cause, death or serious bodily injury to persons, substantial damage to public

---

[1]   For broader discussion of terrorism and cyberspace, see Ben Saul and Kathleen Heath, 'Cyber Terrorism and the Use of the Internet for Terrorist Purposes', in Nicholas Tsagourias and Russell Buchan, eds, *Research Handbook on International Law and Cyberspace* (Edward Elgar, 2nd edn, 2021) [hereinafter *Research Handbook on International Law and Cyberspace*], 204–29.

or private property, the economy, or the environment, or serious disruption of public services and that are undertaken with the intent to spread fear in civilian populations or to compel a government, a civilian population, or an international organization to take or abstain from specific acts or courses of action.[2]

The lack of incidents of cyber terrorism does not mean that terrorists will never use ICTs to cause death, injury, or significant damage to frighten civilians or intimidate governments. Public officials and cybersecurity experts warn that terrorists will eventually add cyberattacks to their arsenal. This possibility means that understanding the law applicable to cyber terrorism is important.

4.2 Cyber terrorism and criminal law

In domestic law, countries criminalize specific acts of terrorism, the provision of material support for terrorists, and the incitement or encouragement of terrorism (Section 4.2.1). States deploy international law, especially treaties, in implementing a criminal-law approach against terrorism (Section 4.2.2). Acts of cyber terrorism could fall within general terrorist offences in domestic criminal codes and anti-terrorism treaties or under criminal offences created for cyber terrorism.

4.2.1 Criminalizing acts of, support for, and glorification and incitement of terrorism

Most countries have criminal offences in domestic law specific to terrorism that could apply to cyber terrorism.[3] To illustrate, in US criminal law, a cyberattack against an electrical power grid would constitute 'international terrorism' if it:

- Endangers human life (e.g., by harming hospital patients);
- Violates US criminal law (e.g., the Computer Fraud and Abuse Act);
- Intends to intimidate or coerce a civilian population or influence government policy through intimidation or coercion; and

---

[2] Report of the International Law Association Study Group on Cybersecurity, Terrorism, and International Law (July 2016), 25.

[3] Governments can also apply cybercrime law to acts of cyber terrorism, as well as other relevant criminal laws (Chapter 3).

- Occurs primarily outside the United States or transcends national boundaries concerning the means used or where the perpetrators operate (e.g., use of the internet) (18 USC, sec. 2331(1)).

Similarly, under Israel's counterterrorism law adopted in 2016, a cyber incident constitutes terrorism when the perpetrator (1) commits a criminal offence; (2) with a political, religious, nationalistic, or ideological motive; (3) with the intent to incite public fear or panic or coerce a governmental entity; and (4) causes severe harm to people, personal freedom, public safety, or health; severe damage to property or religious sites; or severe harm or disturbance to infrastructure, systems, or essential services.

Some countries have created criminal offences specifically to address cyber terrorism. Under the UK's Terrorism Act (2000), the definition of terrorism includes acts designed to interfere seriously with or disrupt an electronic system with the intent to influence the government or to intimidate the public with the purpose of advancing a political, religious, racial, or ideological cause (art. 1(2)(e)). India's Information Technology Act (2000) criminalizes acts (1) undertaken with the intent to threaten the Indian state or strike terror in the people; (2) that deny access to any person authorized to access computers, attempt to penetrate or access computers without authorization, or introduce malware into computers; and (3) through such conduct cause death or injuries to persons, damage or destroy property, disrupt supplies essential to the life of the community, or adversely affect critical infrastructure (sec. 66F).

The criminalization of the provision of material support for terrorist acts or groups is also relevant to cyber terrorism. Generally, the laws criminalizing such support are not specific to cyber terrorism but can apply to cyber support for terrorist activities. Material support could include providing ICT services for terrorists to use in training for, planning, and executing attacks. Pakistan's Prevention of Electronic Crimes Ordinance (2009) defines 'cyber terrorism' to include the 'terrorist act' of using computers to aid the commission of an act of violence against Pakistan (sec. 17). Some countries connect the criminal law on material support for terrorism with the law on cybercrime. The United States criminalizes providing material support or resources for specific terrorist acts or to designated foreign terrorist organizations (18 USC, secs 2339A and 2339B). Such support can include provision of cyber-based resources, equipment, training, services, and expert advice and assistance (18 USC, sec. 2339A(b)). The criminalization of material support for terrorist acts also includes providing support for acts that violate US cybercrime law (18 USC, sec. 2339A(a)). Thus, the United States criminalizes the provision of material support for acts of terrorism that violate the US Computer Fraud and Abuse Act.

Laws criminalizing material support for terrorism have generated controversies. Countries that broadly define terrorism widen the scope of activities that criminal laws on material support for terrorism can reach, such as political speech. Tensions between criminalizing material support for terrorism and political engagement also arise in states that protect freedom of expression. In *Holder v. Humanitarian Law Project* (561 US 1 (2010)), the US Supreme Court addressed whether, under constitutional protections for freedom of speech, the government could criminalize speech acts by a non-governmental organization – training in international humanitarian law provided to terrorist groups – as material support for terrorism. The court held that applying the material-support law did not violate the Constitution because judicial deference to the political branches was necessary concerning whether such speech acts aided terrorists. Terrorist use of US-based social media also triggered controversies over whether the companies were providing material support to terrorist organizations. Under a law that allows victims of international terrorism to sue those responsible, relatives of US nationals killed by terrorist groups sued social media companies in US courts for providing such support. Although unsuccessful, the suits highlighted how terrorists exploit the internet without engaging in cyberattacks.

Some countries have criminalized speech that glorifies, incites, or encourages terrorism. The 11 September 2001 terrorist attacks increased concerns about glorification, incitement, and encouragement of terrorism. In Resolution 1624 (2005), the Security Council called upon UN members to 'prohibit by law incitement to commit a terrorist act or acts' (para. 1(a)). The UK criminalized the publication of statements intended to encourage or induce members of the public to commit, prepare, or institute acts of terrorism, including statements that glorify the commission or preparation of terrorist acts (Terrorism Act (2006), sec. 1). Israel criminalized incitement to terrorism and other acts demonstrating solidarity with a terrorist organization or act of terrorism – a response, in part, to online activities supporting, inciting, and enabling acts of terrorism against

Israel (Counter-Terrorism Law (2016)). These types of criminal laws would apply to statements glorifying, inciting, or encouraging acts of cyber terrorism.

As with criminal laws on material support for terrorism, the criminalization of the glorification, incitement, or encouragement of terrorism has raised concerns that these laws infringe on civil and political rights, especially freedom of expression. UN Secretary-General Kofi Annan captured these worries in 2003 when he opposed using the 'terrorism' label 'to demonize political opponents, to throttle freedom of speech and the press, and to delegitimize legitimate political grievances'.[4] In 2016, the UN's special rapporteur on the right to freedom of opinion and expression highlighted the 'uptick in legislation designated to combat terrorism' that contained broad, ambiguous provisions enabling 'punishment of expression that should not be subject to restriction' (UN Doc. A/71/373, para. 14). This trend has continued and forms part of the global rise of digital authoritarianism (Sections 2.1.2, 2.1.3, and 4.4.1).

However, democracies that value freedom of expression and criminalize glorification, incitement, and encouragement of terrorism struggle with balancing these objectives. The European Court of Human Rights has decided cases involving domestic laws criminalizing glorification, incitement, and encouragement of terrorism. In *Leroy v. France* (No. 36109/03, ECtHR (2008)), a cartoonist challenged his conviction for condoning terrorism for publishing a cartoon after the 11 September 2001 terrorist attacks as a violation of the right to freedom of expression protected by the European Convention of Human Rights. The French court held that the cartoon glorified the terrorist violence against the United States. The European Court of Human Rights upheld the conviction, finding that France had legitimate aims in protecting public safety and preventing disorder or crime and that the law's interference with Leroy's freedom of expression was necessary in a democratic society.

4.2.2   International law and the criminalization of terrorism

States have used international law in implementing the criminal-law approach against terrorism. Since the 1960s, states have adopted treaties

---

[4]   *Statement of Kofi Annan to the 20 January Security Council Ministerial Meeting on Terrorism*, 20 January 2003.

that require states parties to criminalize specific terrorist offences, take jurisdiction over the offences, and engage in law-enforcement cooperation in connection with suspected commission of the offences. This approach resembles the strategy used in cybercrime treaties (Section 3.3.3) in harmonizing the jurisdictional, substantive, and procedural aspects of national criminal law and strengthening law-enforcement cooperation. None of the anti-terrorism treaties focuses on cyber terrorism. However, a terrorist cyberattack could constitute an offence in some anti-terrorism treaties if the attack:

Terrorist offences against air and maritime transportation

- Jeopardizes aircraft safety, the safety of persons or property in an aircraft, or order and discipline onboard an aircraft (Convention on Offences and Certain Other Acts Committed on Board Aircraft (1963), art. 1);
- Seizes or exercises control of an aircraft (Convention for the Suppression of Unlawful Seizure of Aircraft (1970), art. 1; and Protocol Supplemental to the Convention for the Suppression of Unlawful Seizure of Aircraft (2010), art. II);
- Destroys, damages, or interferes with air navigation facilities, thus endangering in-flight aircraft safety (Convention for the Suppression of Unlawful Acts against the Safety of Civil Aviation (1971), art. 1; and Convention on the Suppression of Unlawful Acts Relating to International Civil Aviation (2010), art. 1.1(d));
- Destroys, seriously damages, or disrupts facilities or services at an airport serving international civil aviation (Protocol for the Suppression of Unlawful Acts of Violence at Airports Serving International Civil Aviation (1988), art. II); or
- Destroys, seriously damages, or seriously interferes with maritime navigational facilities in a manner likely to endanger the safety of ship navigation (Convention for the Suppression of Unlawful Acts against the Safety of Maritime Navigation (1988), art. 3.1(e)).

Terrorist offences against infrastructure

- Places on a fixed platform on the continental shelf a device likely to endanger the platform's safety (Protocol for the Suppression of

Unlawful Acts against the Safety of Fixed Platforms Located on the Continental Shelf (1988), art. 2.1(d));

• Causes death, serious bodily injury, or extensive property destruction to a place of public use, government facility, public transportation system, or infrastructure facility by using a weapon or device designed, or that has the capability, to cause such consequences through explosive or incendiary means or through release, dissemination, or impact of toxic chemicals, biological agents, radiation, or radioactive material (International Convention for the Suppression of Terrorist Bombings (1997), arts 2.1 and 3.1); or

• Damages a nuclear facility in a manner that releases, or risks releasing, radioactive material (International Convention for the Suppression of Acts of Nuclear Terrorism (2005), art. 2.1(b)).

Other terrorist offences

• Constitutes a violent attack on the official premises, private accommodations, or means of transport of an internationally protected person (e.g., a diplomat) that endangers the person (Convention on the Prevention and Punishment of Crimes against Internationally Protected Persons, including Diplomatic Agents (1973), art. 2.1(b)); or

• Involves a terrorist offence defined under an anti-terrorism treaty that is facilitated by funds provided or collected with the intent that the funds be used, or with knowledge that the funds would be used, to commit the offence (Convention on the Suppression of the Financing of Terrorism (1999), art. 2(1)).

States have also adopted regional anti-terrorism treaties, and, like the multilateral treaties, none of the regional agreements are specific to cyber terrorism. The regional agreements also use the criminal-law approach to harmonize jurisdictional, substantive, and procedural criminal law and strengthen law-enforcement cooperation. Often, the regional treaties incorporate the offences in the multilateral anti-terrorism treaties and require or encourage countries to ratify them. The Association of Southeast Asian Nations Convention on Counter-Terrorism (2007) encourages states parties to cooperate on, among other things, cyber terrorism, but it does not define cyber terrorism or make it a specific offence.[5] The Shanghai Cooperation Organization's Agreement on Cooperation in the Field of International Information Security (2008) identifies 'information terrorism' – defined as any use of, or an attack on, the 'information space' for terrorist purposes – as a threat and commits states parties to cooperate on countering it. However, the agreement does not require states parties to harmonize criminal law on information terrorism.

After India proposed a comprehensive agreement on international terrorism in 1996, the UN held negotiations on a general anti-terrorism treaty. However, no agreement has been reached because of disagreements about the definition of terrorism and the treaty's scope of application. The agreed part of the definition of international terrorism in the draft text of the Comprehensive Convention on International Terrorism (UN Doc. A/37/57 (2002)) provides:

> Any person commits an offence within the meaning of the present Convention if that person, by any means, unlawfully and intentionally, causes:
> (a) Death or serious bodily injury to any person; or
> (b) Serious damage to public or private property, including a place of public use, a State or government facility, a public transportation system, an infrastructure facility or to the environment; or
> (c) Damage to property, places, facilities or systems referred to in paragraph 1(b) of the present article resulting or likely to result in major economic loss; when the purpose of the conduct, by its nature or context, is to intimidate a population, or to compel a Government or an international organization to do or to abstain from doing any act (art. 2(1)).

Cyber terrorism could fall within this provision because a person can commit the offences listed by 'any means'. In addition, it includes damage to telecommunications and information networks in the offence because the draft convention defines 'infrastructure facility' to include such networks. So, the draft convention's definition of international terrorism covers both the use of cyber technologies and damage to cyber assets.

The failure to agree on a definition of international terrorism suggests that states have not developed general and consistent state practice supported by the sense of legal obligation needed to define such terrorism under

---

[5]   For a regional perspective on cybersecurity in Asia, see Hitoshi Nasu, 'Cyber Security in the Asia-Pacific', in *Research Handbook on International Law and Cyberspace*, 563–80.

customary international law. However, the UN's Special Tribunal for Lebanon, established to investigate the assassination of Lebanese political officials, held that customary international law recognized a crime of international terrorism in peacetime composed of three elements:

> (i) the perpetration of a criminal act (such as murder, kidnapping, hostage-taking, arson, and so on), or threatening such an act; (ii) the intent to spread fear among the population (which would generally entail the creation of public danger) or directly or indirectly coerce a national or international authority to take some action, or to refrain from taking it; (iii) when the act involves a transnational element (STL-11-01/1/AC/R176*bis* (2011), para. 85).

This ruling was praised for being the first time an international legal body stated that customary law contains the crime of international terrorism. The ruling was also criticized, including the assertion that it 'has scant empirical grounding in state practice, its reasoning is poorly substantiated, and it ultimately plays fast and loose with custom formation'.[6] Leaving aside this controversy, the purported customary crime of international terrorism is broad enough to encompass cyber terrorism. Acts of cyber terrorism will usually involve the perpetration of criminal offences (e.g., unauthorized access to computer devices) with transnational elements (e.g., internet use) undertaken to spread fear in the population or coerce a government.

In certain contexts, international law seeks to make sure that perpetrators of certain crimes have nowhere to hide from justice. The oldest example is the authority that international law gives every country to prosecute and punish persons suspected of piracy committed anywhere in the world. The principle of universal jurisdiction could apply to cyber operations that 'constitute crimes under international law subject to the universality principle', including cyberattacks conducted to 'incite terror among the civilian population' during armed conflict and 'acquire the names of individuals registered as a certain race in a State census in order to engage in genocide'.[7]

---

[6]   Ben Saul, 'Legislating from a Radical Hague: The United Nations Special Tribunal for Lebanon Invents an International Crime of Transnational Terrorism', *Leiden Journal of International Law* 24 (2011): 677–700, 678.

[7]   Michael N. Schmitt, gen. ed., *Tallinn Manual 2.0 on the International Law Applicable to Cyber Operations* (CUP, 2nd edn, 2017) [hereinafter *Tallinn Manual 2.0*], 60 and 66.

A number of multilateral anti-terrorism treaties contain a form of universal jurisdiction in requiring states parties to prosecute suspected offenders found in their territories – regardless of where the terrorist offence was committed – or extradite the suspects to a state party that has jurisdiction over the offence. For example, the International Convention for the Suppression of Terrorist Bombings provides that the state party where 'the alleged offender is present shall, … if it does not extradite that person, be obliged, without exception whatsoever and whether or not the offence was committed in its territory, to submit the case without undue delay to its competent authorities for the purpose of prosecution' (art. 8). An act of cyber terrorism that fell within the scope of an anti-terrorism treaty with a prosecute-or-extradite obligation could be subject to this form of universal jurisdiction.

4.2.3 Criminal law, terrorism, and cyber terrorism

Although countries use criminal law against terrorism, the effectiveness of creating criminal offences and punishing perpetrators has been questioned. Counterterrorism experts argue that deterrence, including the threat of criminal sanctions, does not work against terrorists. Thus, the criminal law on terrorism that could apply to cyber terrorism is not the reason why cyber terrorism remains a speculative threat. The lack of cyber terrorism has more to do with terrorists lacking the technical capability and political incentives to launch cyberattacks. If such calculations change as terrorist strategies and tactics evolve, then criminal law on terrorism is unlikely to protect societies from cyber terrorism. Like cybercriminals, cyber terrorists could frustrate criminal law's application, by using ICTs to complicate attribution, and exploit gaps in the enforcement of criminal law to undermine efforts to prosecute and punish perpetrators.

One of the transformative impacts of the terrorist attacks on 11 September 2001 was counterterrorism policy's shift from relying primarily on criminal law towards strategies that would protect societies against terrorist attacks and prevent such attacks. Achieving protection and prevention involved taking policy in directions that do not require additional development of criminal law on terrorism. The next two sections explore the policy and legal aspects of the moves in counterterrorism towards protection (Section 4.3) and prevention (Section 4.4) and the implications of these moves for addressing cyber terrorism.

4.3   Protecting critical infrastructure from terrorism

Counterterrorism policies, especially after 11 September 2001, have stressed protecting against terrorist attacks that criminal-law approaches do not deter. Critical-infrastructure protection (CIP) has been prominent in this shift given the damage and disruption that terrorist attacks against critical infrastructure, such as energy production facilities, could create.[8] The threat of cyber terrorism has expanded CIP efforts to include strengthening the cybersecurity of critical infrastructure. The emphasis on protecting critical infrastructure from cyber terrorism connects to the cyber-defence approach and its 'all hazards' strategy of hardening the target against cyber threats regardless of source (Sections 1.2 and 3.2.5).

4.3.1   Critical-infrastructure protection and domestic law

Countries seek to improve critical-infrastructure cybersecurity through policy strategies and legal measures. The mix of policy and law within different countries reflects various factors, including how governments define critical infrastructure and what proportion of critical infrastructure is operated by the public or private sector. For years, proposals in the United States for legal mandates to strengthen critical-infrastructure cybersecurity failed because of political and private-sector opposition. Instead, the US government collaborated with private-sector actors to develop the Framework for Improving Critical Infrastructure Cybersecurity in 2014 to help operators of critical infrastructure conduct voluntary risk assessments to guide better cybersecurity policies and practices. In addition, the United States created legal protections to provide incentives for critical-infrastructure operators to share cybersecurity information with government agencies, such as information about current cyber threats and ICT vulnerabilities.

By contrast, other countries have imposed legal mandates on operators of critical infrastructure to strengthen cybersecurity. In its Security of Critical Infrastructure Act (2018), Australia created a legally binding framework for managing national security risks associated with critical infrastructure. The legislation requires owners and operators of critical

---

[8]   See also the discussion about the threat that cybercriminal activities, especially ransomware attacks, pose to critical infrastructure in Section 3.3.4.

infrastructure in the electricity, gas, water, and maritime port sectors to provide information for a register of critical-infrastructure assets, respond to government requests for information, comply with government orders to take or avoid certain actions, and cooperate with government assessments of national security risks within critical-infrastructure assets. Although the act is not specific to cybersecurity, its provisions encompass cybersecurity within Australia's 'all hazards' approach to national security risks associated with critical infrastructure. In 2020, the Australian government proposed new legislation to expand the critical-infrastructure sectors regulated and better 'protect Australia's critical infrastructure from all hazards, including the dynamic and potentially catastrophic cascading threats enabled by cyber attacks'.[9] The proposed legislation would create cybersecurity obligations to implement protective measures, share information with the government, and comply with government efforts to disrupt and respond to cyber threats to critical infrastructure.

Ransomware attacks by cybercriminals against critical infrastructure (Section 3.3.4) has produced heightened interest in using law more to improve critical-infrastructure cybersecurity. Despite claims to the contrary, these ransomware attacks were not cyber terrorism. But they exposed the vulnerabilities of critical-infrastructure sectors to malign cyber operations and the need for better 'all hazards' cyber defences. In the United States, ransomware attacks against companies operating oil pipelines and food-production facilities in 2021 produced a surge of interest in imposing legal mandates on private-sector operators of critical infrastructure to achieve better defences against cybersecurity threats. The proliferation of ransomware attacks also prompted Australia to begin exploring options for legal reforms in 2021 to strengthen cybersecurity in critical infrastructure and across the Australian economy.

4.3.2 Critical-infrastructure protection and international law

Terrorist cyberattacks against critical infrastructure would bring cybercrime treaties (Section 3.3.3) and anti-terrorism treaties (Section 4.2.2) into play,[10] but these treaties do not focus on protecting critical infra-

---

[9]   *Protecting Critical Infrastructure and Systems of National Significance* (Consultation Paper, August 2020).

[10] Depending on the nature of the attack, the critical infrastructure targeted, and the impact, a terrorist cyberattack could constitute an armed attack

structure before cyberattacks happen. CIP efforts tend to be domestically focused because states can do much to protect critical infrastructure against terrorism without international cooperation. However, the shift in counterterrorism policy towards protection has caused such cooperation on CIP to increase.

States use existing treaties not specific to CIP to strengthen the security of critical infrastructure against terrorism, including cyber threats. Under the UN Charter, the Security Council's Counter-Terrorism Committee has addressed CIP in working with UN members on implementation of Security Council resolutions on terrorism. Regional organizations, such as the Association of South East Asian Nations, and security bodies, such as NATO, devote attention to CIP. International organizations, treaty regimes, and cooperative mechanisms relevant to critical-infrastructure sectors – such as nuclear energy, transportation, and communication satellites – work on cybersecurity. CIP cooperation encourages states to strengthen domestic cyber defences through, for example, creating computer-incident response teams, sharing information between the public and private sectors, assisting companies that operate critical infrastructure, and facilitating the flow of cybersecurity information and best practices between countries.

Treaty law specific to critical-infrastructure cybersecurity is, at present, limited in scope and general in nature. Members of the Shanghai Cooperation Organization agreed to cooperate on information security relevant to critical infrastructure. The African Union's Convention on Cybersecurity and Personal Data Protection requires state parties to adopt national cybersecurity policies that include strengthening critical-infrastructure cybersecurity. The EU requires members to improve their cybersecurity capabilities and to mandate operators of essential services – such as energy, transport, banking, health, and digital infrastructure – to adopt appropriate cybersecurity measures and report cyber incidents to governmental authorities.

---

under international law, triggering the right to use force in self-defence, or it might violate international humanitarian law during armed conflict. See Chapter 6.

4.4   Counterterrorism, electronic surveillance, and cybersecurity

In addition to turning counterterrorism towards protection strategies, the 11 September 2001 attacks provided incentives for governments to prevent terrorism. The prevention imperative had significant impact in connection with government powers to conduct electronic surveillance. Governments expanded their surveillance powers to identify and disrupt terrorist activities before attacks happened. With the proliferation of digital ICTs linked through the internet, expanded surveillance powers provided governments with access to communication infrastructures, networks, devices, and services on a massive scale. This level of government intrusion created fears that expansive surveillance made cyberspace and ICTs insecure, and such cyber insecurity threatened individual rights, such as privacy and freedom of expression.

These concerns reached fever pitch when Edward Snowden, a contractor for the US National Security Agency, started leaking classified documents in 2013 primarily about US and UK electronic surveillance programmes targeting terrorism and other national security threats. Snowden's disclosures sparked debates about how to balance enhanced government surveillance authority with legal protections for individual rights. However, the episode did not produce, as many hoped, a fundamental paring back of government surveillance powers in the cyber age. Some democracies, including the United States and the UK, made changes, but, globally, government surveillance powers expanded after Snowden's leaks, fuelling the rise of digital authoritarianism and digital repression.

4.4.1   Counterterrorism, electronic surveillance, and domestic law

Countries have policies and laws that authorize and regulate domestic government surveillance for law enforcement (Section 3.2.3), counterintelligence (Section 5.3.2), and counterterrorism purposes. Regulation of domestic surveillance can involve constitutional law, statutes, and policies guiding government agencies. For surveillance inside the United States, the mixture involves the Fourth Amendment to the Constitution on government searches and seizures, the regulation of domestic surveillance under the Foreign Intelligence Surveillance Act (FISA), and executive orders applicable to counterterrorism and counterintelligence activities. Domestic law on surveillance differs among countries based on various factors, including whether a state is democratic or authoritarian, the national security risks it faces, how it protects individual rights, and the human and technological capabilities of its law enforcement and intelligence agencies.

Historically, governments have increased their surveillance activities and their legal authority to conduct surveillance in response to heightened national security threats. After the 11 September 2001 attacks, many countries expanded their surveillance powers for counterterrorism purposes. Perhaps the most famous expansion was the USA PATRIOT Act adopted by the United States in October 2001. As Section 4.2 discussed, many countries exploited the 11 September attacks to increase surveillance against terrorism broadly defined. This interest in greater surveillance powers and capabilities arose during the first decade of the twenty-first century, when growing internet access, smartphones, other mobile technologies, and new platforms (e.g., social media) revolutionized communication. Governments used this revolution to justify increasing surveillance activities, expanding the scope of surveillance laws, and changing how they conducted surveillance. The secrecy under which counterterrorism strategies and surveillance programmes operate often make oversight of government actions difficult and non-transparent.

Concerns about the scale, sophistication, legality, impact, and oversight of post-11 September counterterrorism surveillance emerged in democracies before Snowden. The transformation in electronic communications, combined with expanded and aggressively interpreted surveillance laws, produced fears that governments were engaged in mass surveillance without adequate rules to protect privacy or sufficient oversight to ensure democratic accountability. Leaks to the press in 2005 exposed a surveillance programme created after 11 September under which the US government collected the content of electronic communications of US nationals in ways that federal law did not authorize. The leaks forced President George W. Bush to ask Congress to create new surveillance authority responsive to the terrorist threat in the context of cyber communications, which Congress did by amending FISA in 2008.

Snowden's disclosures proved more explosive because they exposed the surveillance activities of democratic countries, especially the United States and the UK. Snowden's revelations raised questions about domestic laws that authorized – or that governments claimed permitted – surveillance on the scale, intensity, and secrecy revealed in the leaked documents. The disclosures also prompted examination of surveillance laws under human rights obligations that states have under international law (Section 4.4.2). The debates in democracies were not identical given differences in political and legal systems, technological capabilities, and geopolitical status. However, common themes included heightened scrutiny of surveillance powers, increased transparency about surveillance policies, and reform of surveillance laws.

As Snowden's main target, the United States provides a prominent example of what happened in democratic countries in the wake of revelations about surveillance in the cyber age. The leaks sparked political debate that involved government officials, civil society organizations, companies, politicians, and academics. Responses from US officials shed light on surveillance policies and practices. President Barack Obama instituted policy changes to provide more transparency and oversight concerning surveillance. Congress changed federal law concerning the surveillance programmes that caused the most serious controversies.

The political debate, policy changes, and legal reforms ended the programme that collected telephone metadata (e.g., telephone numbers used in making calls) because it had a weak legal justification under the USA PATRIOT Act and demonstrated no utility in counterterrorism investigations. Policy and law concerning surveillance conducted in the United States against targets located in other countries (e.g., intercepting electronic mail to and from the United States) conducted under the 2008 amendment to FISA also changed, but not dramatically. Congress extensively debated this amendment before it was enacted, which made its legal foundation stronger. In addition, the counterterrorism and foreign intelligence value of the surveillance conducted under that FISA amendment was significant.

The scale, intensity, and variety of surveillance revealed by Snowden caused concerns that electronic communications, ICTs, and networks were insecure and vulnerable to government manipulation and access. The 'offensive' use of cyber technologies by governments to prevent terrorism produced 'defensive' reactions by users against the cyber insecurity that extensive surveillance created. Law-abiding citizens and terrorists turned to encryption as one way to counter government surveillance.

This embrace of encryption meant that the going-dark problem could affect counterterrorism efforts to identify threats and intervene before terrorists attacked. The threat that encryption poses to counterterrorism echoes problems that encryption creates for law enforcement concerning cybercrime (Section 3.2.4). For cybersecurity experts, adding counter-terrorism as a reason to weaken encryption did not reduce the danger that counter-encryption measures would make cyberspace less secure for everyone, not just the bad guys. Snowden stoked these controversies by leaking information about US efforts to defeat encryption used by foreign governments and terrorists.

While democracies struggled with surveillance policy and law in respond-ing to Snowden, the affair gave authoritarian countries additional motivation to achieve cyber sovereignty, including through expanded sur-veillance of domestic online activities. In 2018, five years after Snowden began leaking documents, Freedom House warned that internet freedom continued declining and that digital authoritarianism was increasing. Broad definitions of terrorism helped justify extensive surveillance of domestic communication. In 2020, Freedom House reported that per-vasive online surveillance contributed to the global increase in digital repression – government use of information obtained through surveil-lance to deter, limit, censor, silence, and prohibit political speech and association deemed hostile to state interests and social order. The rise of digital authoritarianism and digital repression demonstrates that many countries have exploited the threat of terrorism to use domestic policy and law to create and sustain pervasive surveillance systems in which individual rights, such as privacy and freedom of expression, have no meaningful protections.

4.4.2   Counterterrorism, electronic surveillance, and international law

Well before Snowden, the convergence of post-11 September coun-terterrorism strategies and the communication revolution associated with digital, internet-linked ICTs produced alarm that counterterrorism surveillance violated international human rights law.[11] Snowden's dis-

---

[11]   For broader analysis of international human rights, see David P. Fidler, 'Cyberspace and Human Rights', in *Research Handbook on International Law and Cyberspace*, 130–51.

closures supercharged this debate. This controversy involved more than counterterrorism surveillance because it also provoked discussion about whether, in the cyber age, international human rights law places limits on government espionage (Section 5.2.3). Even so, governmental reliance on counterterrorism as a justification for extensive surveillance was prominent in the Snowden-triggered controversies about surveillance and international human rights law.

As with much human rights activity, the UN was a prominent forum for addressing the human rights implications of the surveillance programmes that Snowden disclosed. The General Assembly adopted a resolution on the right to privacy in the digital age, UN human rights officials compiled reports, and the Human Rights Council established a special rapporteur on the right to privacy. The Snowden leaks prompted activities within regional human rights regimes, including the American Convention on Human Rights and the European Convention for Human Rights. The European Union forced the US government to agree to stronger privacy protections for digital data flowing from EU members to the United States. The angst about counterterrorism efforts 'going dark' because of encryption garnered attention as well, with a UN special rapporteur emphasizing how encryption provides 'individuals and groups with a zone of privacy online to hold opinions and exercise freedom of expression without arbitrary and unlawful interference or attacks' (UN Doc. A/HRC/29/32 (2015), para. 16).

International human rights activity on surveillance in the wake of Snowden affected policy and law in countries differently. The United States stressed that its obligations under the International Covenant on Civil and Political Rights (ICCPR) did not apply to its surveillance against targets outside the United States. In conducting surveillance against foreign targets, the United States argued that it had no obligations under the ICCPR's privacy provisions. In US debates about domestic surveillance, the ICCPR played no role. By contrast, the UK faced litigation over its surveillance laws and policies before British courts under the Human Rights Act and before the European Court on Human Rights under the European Convention on Human Rights. As the rise of digital authoritarianism and digital repression signals, authoritarian countries have paid little, if any, attention to obligations they have under international human rights law concerning electronic surveillance.

4.5   International law and state responsibility for combating terrorism

Under the UN Charter, Security Council decisions are legally binding on UN members (art. 25). In Resolution 1373 (2001), adopted after the 11 September 2001 terrorist attacks, the Security Council imposed binding obligations on UN members to implement certain counterterrorism measures, such as taking the necessary steps to prevent the commission of terrorist acts and strengthen various national and international actions against terrorism. The resolution does not mention cyber terrorism, but its obligations apply to cyber terrorism because the Security Council did not restrict the resolution to traditional forms of terrorism. In the event of a cyber terrorist incident, governments and the UN would likely refer to Resolution 1373 (2001).

More broadly, general principles of international law on state responsibility require states not to engage in internationally wrongful acts and to ensure that activities within their territories do not cause damage in other states (Section 3.3.4). A state's use of terrorist proxies to attack other states would violate these principles. Under the international law on state responsibility, a state is legally responsible for the actions of non-governmental actors, such as terrorists, when that 'person or group of persons is in fact acting on the instructions of, or under the direction or control of, that State in carrying out the conduct' (UN Doc. A/56/10 (2001), 47, art. 8). This effective-control test sets the bar high for attributing non-state actor behaviour to a state, which has contributed to controversies concerning terrorism. Some states victimized by terrorism, such as Israel and the United States, have claimed a right under international law to use force in self-defence against or within states unwilling or unable to act against terrorists operating in their territories.[12] This unwilling-or-unable standard has been controversial because it is not consistent with the effective-control test.

Cyber technologies create difficulties for applying the international law on state responsibility to cyber terrorism. Terrorists could use the internet

---

[12]   See the discussion of the possible emergence of the unwilling-or-unable standard in the context of addressing cybercrime against critical infrastructure in Section 3.3.4. On the international law on the right to use force in self-defence, see Section 6.3.

to launch cyberattacks from, and route attacks through, different geographical locations, making it difficult to pinpoint the origin of the attacks for purposes of attributing state responsibility. Even if such attribution proves possible, the effective-control test means that a state's 'general support for or encouragement of a non-State actor or its cyber operations is insufficient' to establish state responsibility, and even 'the provision of malware by a State to a non-State actor does not amount, without more, to effective control over operations conducted by the group using that malware'.[13]

If a state has exercised effective control over an act of cyber terrorism, then the victim state must comply with the international legal rules on responding to such an internationally wrongful act. The injured state could try to bring the non-state actors to justice within their national legal systems by using anti-terrorism treaties (Section 4.2.2) or treaties on cybercrime, extradition, and mutual legal assistance (Sections 3.3.2 and 3.3.3). If the injured state wants to act against the state responsible for the act of cyber terrorism, then it could engage in retorsion – legal but unfriendly actions – or use countermeasures proportional to 'the injury suffered, taking into account the gravity of the internationally wrongful act and the rights in question' (UN Doc. A/56/10 (2001), 134, art. 51). An injured state could respond by using force in self-defence against the responsible state if a terrorist cyberattack caused damage sufficient to constitute an armed attack under international law. However, many possible acts of cyber terrorism might not trigger the victim's right to use force in self-defence, leaving retorsion and countermeasures as the responses that an injured state could use against acts of cyber terrorism conducted under the effective control of another state.

A state would also commit an internationally wrongful act by tolerating terrorist activities, including cyber terrorism, undertaken from its territory that cause damage in other states. Anti-terrorism treaties (Section 4.2.2) require states parties to prohibit persons or groups from using their respective territories to commit the terrorist offences criminalized in the treaties. This counterterrorism obligation connects with the due-diligence principle in international law that requires states to act when they know, or should know, that non-state actors in their territories are causing

---

[13] *Tallinn Manual 2.0*, 97.

damage in other states, a principle also discussed in connection with cybercrime (Section 3.3.4).

In 2021, the government of Afghanistan fell to the Taliban, ending a twenty-year effort at nation-building by the United States and its NATO allies. Terrorist violence perpetrated during and after the withdrawal of foreign nationals from Afghanistan provoked concerns about a resurgence of terrorism, including the possibility that groups, such as Al Qaeda and the Islamic State, might operate from Afghan territory and exploit the humiliating defeat suffered by Western countries. These concerns highlight the controversies discussed above about state responsibility for terrorist activities and about the right to use force in self-defence to respond to or prevent terrorist attacks. Whether terrorist groups again operate from Afghanistan and attack targets in other countries, as Al Qaeda did before the 11 September 2001 attacks, is unclear. The anxiety about a new surge of terrorism includes worries that terrorists will continue to exploit the internet for propaganda, recruiting, radicalization, and fundraising to plan and execute attacks. Whether any new wave of terrorism involves cyber terrorism remains to be seen.

PART III

Cybersecurity and state actors:
Espionage and war in cyberspace

5   Cyber espionage

In their competition for power and influence, states have always exploited new communication technologies to engage in espionage. The embrace by intelligence agencies of cyber espionage is, thus, unsurprising. However, the internet makes espionage possible on a scale and intensity previously not feasible. That reality is eye opening given how much states have exploited every means of communication to conduct espionage, and it is the source of increasing national security concerns.

For clarity, 'espionage' refers to actions a government takes to obtain information covertly from (1) another government, individuals, or non-governmental entities in foreign countries that possess secret or politically important information (traditional espionage); and (2) companies located in foreign countries (economic espionage). With espionage, state action is the focus, rather than non-state actors – criminals (Chapter 3) and terrorists (Chapter 4).

Edward Snowden's disclosures, discussed in Chapter 4, provided glimpses of the secret world of cyber espionage and of the scale, diversity, and sophistication of US cyber espionage. Other countries have developed such capabilities as well. Government agencies, non-governmental entities, and companies around the world have been, and continue to be, victims of cyber espionage. All nations and societies, even the most powerful and affluent, are vulnerable to this form of espionage. The world learned at the end of 2020 and the start of 2021 that US government agencies and corporations had, once again, been victims of cyber espionage on a significant scale through the SolarWinds and Microsoft Exchange hacks.

Cyber espionage is a critical cybersecurity problem. In many ways, cyber espionage is the most damaging activity in cyberspace from a national security perspective. Although cybercrime continues to grow, it has not created equivalent strategic tensions between states in the manner cyber espionage has done, for example, in US relations with China and Russia.[1] Cyber terrorism remains a possible threat rather than an ongoing problem (Chapter 4). To date, military use of cyber weapons in warfare has been limited (Chapter 6). By contrast, most governments engage in cyber espionage and, in the process, cause damage to the national security, economies, and corporations of other states that creates friction in international relations.

After a closer look at cyber espionage (Section 5.1), this chapter examines how states have treated espionage under international law and whether cyber espionage changes, or should change, how international law applies to espionage (Section 5.2). The next section considers cyber espionage in the context of how states use domestic law to authorize espionage, regulate intelligence activities, and defend against cyber espionage (Section 5.3). The final part analyses how covert cyber operations, which go beyond espionage, affect international and domestic law (Section 5.4).

5.1   The cyber espionage problem

Cyber espionage emerged into an environment that has long lacked effective restraints on spying. Every government prohibits espionage within its territory (Section 5.3.2), but every government spies within the territory of other countries. The ubiquity of spying means that domestic policies and legal prohibitions have no deterrent effect, and that states have little interest in developing international law to regulate espionage.[2] States also have not attempted to retaliate against foreign governments for spying to create deterrence by punishment. With domestic regulation ineffective and deterrence non-existent, countries must rely on defensive strategies to: (1) protect against espionage by restricting access to information to specific people using designated information systems at secure locations; and (2) defend against espionage through counterintelligence activities.

---

[1]   But see the escalating tensions between the United States and Russia over cybercriminal ransomware attacks on critical infrastructure discussed in Section 3.3.4.

[2]   But cyber espionage has stimulated new debates about international law and espionage discussed in Section 5.2.

The internet and increased dependence on cyberspace have provided intelligence agencies with more capabilities, targets, and incentives to engage in spying. Compared with past barriers to entry for conducting large-scale signals intelligence against radio, telephone, and satellite communications, governments can exploit the internet to spy on a scale, speed, intensity, and depth never possible before. The global dissemination of cyber technologies and internet access has democratized the ability to engage in cost-effective, large-scale, and high-tech espionage. Intelligence agencies can also manipulate cyber technologies to make attribution difficult, thus reducing or delaying the political costs of getting caught.

Cyber technologies also make cyber espionage a force multiplier for governments. What intelligence agencies learn in penetrating foreign networks is also valuable for protecting and defending national networks, conducting covert cyber operations (Section 5.4), and making military cyber weapons (Chapter 6). Cyber espionage contributes to the development of 'full spectrum' offensive and defensive cyber capabilities. As such, cyber espionage helps countries embed cyber capabilities into their national security strategies, intelligence calculations, military operations, and economic interests.

Cyberspace also affects the relationship between espionage and crime by creating synergies between them. Distinguishing between hacking for espionage and for crime can be difficult because the techniques are interchangeable, the malware similar, and the targets often the same, especially when spies and crooks go after companies. Governments can also outsource cyber espionage to criminals skilled at internet exploitation. Intelligence agencies also learn from watching how cybercriminals operate.

The deep and intense government interest in cyber espionage underscores the lack of legal rules and deterrence that have long characterized this area. As with other forms of espionage, governments must rely on defensive strategies to combat cyber espionage. This reality elevates the importance of cybersecurity across public and private networks. However, as with cybercrime, cyber espionage incidents continue to highlight problems with cyber defences in government and company networks. These problems undermine defensive strategies designed to protect sensitive information from spies and to disrupt foreign intelligence activities.

The increased interest in international law generated by cyber espionage arises, in part, because deterrence remains non-existent and achieving effective domestic cyber defences proves difficult. In the past, states demonstrated little interest in regulating espionage through international law. This pattern of behaviour has been constant each time new ICTs emerged to provide intelligence agencies with additional capabilities. This chapter analyses whether and how cyber espionage might change this pattern (Sections 5.2.2 and 5.2.3).

5.2   Cyber espionage and international law

5.2.1   The traditional approach to espionage under international law

Historically, international lawyers did not pay much attention to espionage. States did not produce much treaty law relevant to espionage. Treaty law on diplomatic relations contains some rules intended to constrain spying on diplomatic premises and communications. The effectiveness of these rules is questionable, and diplomatic missions have not relied on them to protect their activities from espionage. Pervasive spying by countries against each other meant that state practice did not produce customary international law on espionage. Although countries banned spying in their territories, they authorized their governments to conduct espionage in other nations. Domestic laws across the international system do not reflect general principles that could serve as international legal restrictions on spying. States also did not seriously argue that general principles of international law, especially sovereignty and non-intervention, prohibited or restricted espionage, even when spying caused national security, political, and economic damage to governmental and private-sector activities, capabilities, and interests. Nor did states debate whether specific bodies of international law, such as on human rights or trade, regulated espionage.

In doctrinal terms, this traditional narrative about espionage has two different explanations. Under the first, international law permits spying because it does not regulate espionage. This explanation connects with the proposition that, in the absence of prohibitive or restrictive rules, states are free under international law to behave as they deem necessary and appropriate. This freedom to spy does not always have adverse consequences because espionage is often necessary and appropriate. Information gathered through spying can help reduce the prospects for war, such as providing 'ground truth' during crises or supporting verification of agreements designed to reduce military tensions, such as arms control treaties. The second explanation holds that, through the ubiquitous practice of espionage, states recognize an affirmative right under international law to spy – a right bolstered by how espionage supports other international legal rights, such as a government's right of self-defence against armed attack. Neither governments nor international lawyers have been particularly interested in which of the two explanations is better because both support the conclusion that international law does not regulate espionage in any serious way.

Of more interest is whether the means and methods used to conduct espionage might violate international law. For example, states consider aerial surveillance over their territories by a foreign government without permission to be a violation of sovereignty. Similarly, if spies damage a country's telecommunications system while wiretapping, then that damage could factor into analysing whether the methods used to wiretap violate sovereignty, are an illegal intervention, or constitute an impermissible use for force. If serious enough, such damage could constitute sabotage and would fall under the international law applied to covert actions (Section 5.4). However, spill over from espionage into sabotage does not arise frequently because intelligence agencies have little interest in damaging the human and technological sources used in espionage. Indeed, intelligence agencies have incentives to spy in ways that do not draw attention to their activities.

5.2.2   Cyber espionage and rethinking the traditional approach to espionage under international law

The rise of cyber espionage has stimulated more international legal interest in espionage than was seen historically.[3] This phenomenon developed

---

[3]   See Russell Buchan and Iñaki Navarette, 'Cyber Espionage and International Law', in Nicholas Tsagourias and Russell Buchan, eds, *Research Handbook on International Law and Cyberspace* (Edward Elgar, 2nd edn, 2021) [hereinafter *Research Handbook on International Law and Cyberspace*], 230–51; Asaf Lubin, 'The Liberty to Spy', *Harvard International Law Journal* 61(1) (2020): 185–243; and Russell Buchan, *Cyber Espionage and International Law* (Hart, 2018).

in response to high-profile incidents of traditional and economic espionage conducted through cyber technologies. The most important development in the emergence of this interest was the disclosures that Edward Snowden made starting in 2013 about US cyber espionage programmes, especially the bulk collection of information for intelligence and counterintelligence purposes.[4] Snowden's revelations triggered controversies about cyber espionage across different areas of international law. Damage done to the US government and the private sector by cyber espionage also stimulated debates about whether new international legal rules designed to address cyber espionage should be developed.

The increased international legal interest stimulated by cyber espionage has manifested itself in three approaches:

- Challenging the traditional perspective by arguing that international law, including the law on sovereignty, regulates espionage in more meaningful ways than the traditional perspective acknowledges;
- Arguing that specific bodies of international law that protect human rights (e.g., privacy) and economic rights (e.g., intellectual property) regulate acts of cyber espionage that adversely affect these rights (Section 5.2.3); and
- Asserting that cyber espionage is fundamentally different from earlier types of spying because public and private dependence on cyber technologies makes cyber espionage possible on such a scale, intensity, and severity that states must develop new international law to regulate it.

In analysing cyber espionage, the *Tallinn Manual 2.0 on International Law Applicable to Cyber Operations* (*Tallinn Manual 2.0*) touched on each of these approaches.[5] It reinforced the validity of the traditional perspective by stating that cyber espionage 'does not *per se* violate international law' but 'the method by which it is carried out might do so' (*Tallinn Manual 2.0*, 168). It rejected the proposition that cyber espionage has become so damaging that international law prohibits it generally or when the

---

4   As Chapter 4 analysed, Snowden's disclosures revealed large-scale surveillance undertaken for counterterrorism purposes after the 11 September 2001 attacks. Such counterterrorism surveillance used intelligence capabilities originally designed for espionage and counterintelligence activities.

5   Michael N. Schmitt, gen. ed., *Tallinn Manual 2.0 on the International Law Applicable to Cyber Operations* (CUP, 2nd edn, 2017). For the rest of this chapter, references to the *Tallinn Manual 2.0* appear in the text.

damage crosses a 'threshold of severity' (*Tallinn Manual 2.0*, 169, 170–1). The manual analysed how specific bodies of international law apply to cyber operations, including what impact these regimes have on cyber espionage (*Tallinn Manual 2.0*, 177–300), but it did not conclude that any of these regimes treats cyber espionage differently from pre-cyber spying. The manual acknowledged that states could develop new prohibitions or restrictions on cyber espionage through treaty or customary international law but that, to date, states had not done so (*Tallinn Manual 2.0*, 169).

As the *Tallinn Manual 2.0* reflects, cyber espionage has not caused governments to reinterpret international law to conclude that espionage has been illegal all along. The reciprocal interests that states have long had in not considering espionage illegal *per se* continue undiminished, and perhaps are heightened, in the cyber age. States are free to develop new international law on espionage generally or cyber espionage specifically. However, states have not exhibited serious interest in negotiating treaty law on cyber espionage or collectively changing their behaviour to develop new customary international law.

In this context, the most sustained debates have focused on whether specific bodies of international law regulate cyber espionage. Within these debates, international human rights law and international trade law have garnered the most attention because of the risks that cyber espionage poses to individual and economic rights protected under international law. In both cases, the international legal arguments have hinged on whether treaty obligations binding within sovereign territory apply when states parties conduct espionage in foreign countries.

5.2.3   Cyber espionage, economic cyber espionage, and the extraterritorial application of international law

Generally, obligations that states have under international law have binding effect where states have jurisdiction over the subject matter of the obligations. For example, a state party to a human rights treaty must comply with the treaty concerning individuals within its territory. Similarly, a state party to an international economic agreement that includes protections for intellectual property rights must protect such rights for foreign investors operating in its territory. Espionage is, by definition, an extraterritorial act – a state activity directed at foreign countries, nationals, and companies. Rules of international law not specifically about spying could only regulate espionage if they apply extraterritorially. Cyber espionage has generated controversies about the extraterritorial application of the international law protecting human rights and intellectual property rights.

International human rights

International human rights law has long encountered disagreements about when human rights obligations under treaties or customary international law apply extraterritorially. Many, though not all, states hold that human rights obligations have extraterritorial application when a state subject to such obligations has physical power or effective control over foreign territory or individuals in foreign territory.[6] Acts of espionage, even those undertaken within foreign territory and involving foreign nationals, typically do not require or involve physical power or effective control over foreign territory or individuals. The same is true, and even more so, for cyber espionage. The majority of the international lawyers crafting the *Tallinn Manual 2.0* concluded that, in connection with state cyber operations, 'physical control over territory or the individual is required' before human rights obligations apply extraterritorially (*Tallinn Manual 2.0*, 185). Under this view, international human rights law, including the right to privacy, does not regulate cyber espionage.

However, some international lawyers maintain that human rights obligations apply extraterritorially when a state has non-physical effective power or control over whether an individual can exercise or enjoy a human right. Under this perspective, a state conducting cyber espionage could remotely gain effective power or control over a foreign individual's computer or digital data in ways that could violate the right to privacy. Under this perspective, bulk collection of data produced by foreign nationals in other countries violates the requirement of proportionality that forms part of a lawful search and seizure of information protected by the right to privacy. Accordingly, the extraterritorial application of the right to privacy would prohibit bulk collection of electronically stored or communicated data of foreign individuals. Such extraterritorial

---

6   By contrast, the United States has long maintained that its obligations under the ICCPR, which includes the right to privacy, do not apply extraterritorially, even when the United States has physical power or effective control over foreign nationals outside the United States.

application means that the government engaging in cyber espionage must comply with its human rights obligations on conducting a lawful search and seizure of an individual's information.

In the wake of Snowden's disclosures, especially those concerning bulk collection programmes, support for the extraterritorial application of the right to privacy and other human rights to electronic surveillance, regardless of purpose, was voiced as the UN focused on 'the right to privacy in the digital age' (UN Doc. A/RES/68/167 (2013)). Among other things, the debates produced intergovernmental and non-governmental reports, the appointment of a UN special rapporteur on the right to privacy, litigation under the European Convention on Human Rights, heightened privacy concerns in the EU about the commercial transfer of data from the EU to the United States,[7] and changes in US policy on signals intelligence (Section 5.3.2).

However, this activity did not produce a new consensus among states on the extraterritorial application of human rights obligations. The post-Snowden context has witnessed the rise of digital authoritarianism (Section 4.4.2), which means more countries are infringing the right to privacy domestically in violation of international human rights law. This trend undercuts arguments that states recognize that their international human rights obligations apply extraterritorially and regulate espionage.

The international lawyers crafting the *Tallinn Manual 2.0* could not agree whether international human rights law applies extraterritorially to cyber operations by states 'that do not involve an exercise of physical control' (*Tallinn Manual 2.0*, 185). The majority underscored that 'there is little evidence that when States conduct signals intelligence programmes directed at foreigners in foreign territory, they consider that their activities implicate the international human right to privacy' (*Tallinn Manual 2.0*, 185). The controversy over the extraterritorial application of human

---

[7]   The EU and the United States have had problems, which pre-date the Snowden controversies, over the transfer of data from the EU to the United States. The EU has been concerned that such transfer subjects EU-origin data to US privacy laws that do not protect the data as EU law does. These concerns include how US surveillance laws enforced within the United States affect the privacy of EU nationals. However, these EU–US difficulties do not involve EU opposition to US cyber espionage under international law.

rights law to cyber operations has not generated sufficient interest among states to start negotiating new international legal rules on such extraterritorial application.[8]

Intellectual property rights

A debate about the extraterritorial application of international legal obligations also arose in connection with treaties on trade and investment that protect intellectual property rights. The growing problem of economic cyber espionage produced arguments that members of the World Trade Organization (WTO) engaging in economic cyber espionage against companies located in other WTO members violated WTO rules on the protection of intellectual property rights. Under the Agreement on Trade-Related Aspects of Intellectual Property Rights (TRIPS), WTO members agreed to protect the intellectual property rights of companies from other WTO members established under the domestic law of the member hosting such companies. TRIPS incorporates obligations in treaties on intellectual property rights negotiated before the WTO's creation, including the Paris Convention for the Protection of Industrial Property (1967). These obligations mean, for example, that China must protect the intellectual property rights that US companies establish under Chinese law in setting up operations in China.

With TRIPS, intellectual property rights remain territorial in nature. The Chinese government does not have to recognize and enforce a patent granted by the US government, and *vice versa*. The US and Chinese governments have been in disputes about whether China complies with TRIPS in connection with the intellectual property rights that US companies obtain in China as part of doing business there. However, neither TRIPS nor any intellectual property treaty it incorporates contains any specific provisions that apply its requirements extraterritorially. With economic cyber espionage targeting the intellectual property owned by companies, debates about the extraterritorial application of international

---

[8]   Some countries apply domestic legal protections for individual rights to the extraterritorial activities of intelligence agencies (Section 5.3.1). A country's decision to apply its domestic law to the extraterritorial activities of its intelligence agencies is not necessarily evidence that the country believes that it must apply its obligations under international human rights law extraterritorially to its espionage activities.

human rights obligations are not relevant because human rights law does not protect corporations.

Interpretating TRIPS, or the pre-WTO intellectual property treaties it incorporates, to support the extraterritorial application of these instruments finds no support in how WTO members and the states parties of the incorporated treaties have applied these agreements over more than five decades. For example, the WTO dispute settlement process has been functioning for over 25 years, but no WTO member has used it to claim that economic espionage by another WTO member violates TRIPS or any intellectual property treaty that it incorporates.

In a breakthrough, the United States and China negotiated a non-binding agreement in 2015 that addressed economic cyber espionage in a manner that did not involve the extraterritorial application of existing international legal obligations: 'The United States and China agree that neither country's government will conduct or knowingly support cyber-enabled theft of intellectual property, including trade secrets or other confidential business information, with the intent of providing competitive advantage to companies or commercial sectors' (White House, Fact Sheet, 25 September 2015). This agreement led to similar ones between China and other countries, including Germany and the UK, and a commitment from the major economic powers in the Group of 20 that 'no country should conduct or support ICT-enabled theft of intellectual property, including trade secrets or other confidential business information, with the intent of providing competitive advantages to companies or commercial sectors' (Group of 20 Leaders' Communique, 15–16 November 2015).

Although not binding under international law, such agreements created more international cooperation on economic espionage than had happened before. However, the US–China agreement broke down as Sino-American relations deteriorated over, among other things, US accusations that Chinese technology companies facilitated China's economic cyber espionage against Western corporations. The United States mounted a campaign at home and abroad – the Clean Network Program – to deny Chinese technology companies access to foreign markets for ICT goods and services. The United States accused China of (1) orchestrating the Microsoft Exchange hacking incident that compromised the systems of thousands of companies; and (2) using non-governmental hackers, who also engage in cybercrime, to obtain information from

Western companies. With the world's two strongest powers quarrelling over economic cyber espionage, collective action against such espionage evaporated.

Countries have not used new trade and investment agreements to prohibit or restrict economic espionage or provide that treaty obligations on intellectual property protections have extraterritorial application. Despite identifying economic cyber espionage as a US national security threat, trade and investment treaties negotiated by the United States since the breakdown of the 2015 US–China agreement do not include provisions on economic espionage. The US government claims that the intellectual property provisions in the United States–Mexico–Canada Agreement (USMCA (2018)) contain the most advanced protections for intellectual property rights of any international economic agreement. However, the USMCA does not address economic espionage, nor did the US government's praise for its intellectual property provisions mention such espionage. Similarly, the Economic and Trade Agreement between China and the United States (2020) has no provisions on economic espionage, and the US government's description of this agreement's achievements on intellectual property makes no reference to economic espionage.[9] As commentators noted, the agreement left US concerns about Chinese economic espionage unresolved.

In sum, despite concern about traditional and economic cyber espionage damaging international politics, violating human rights, and destabilizing economic relations, international law on espionage remains unchanged. Espionage, including cyber espionage, does not *per se* violate international law, but the method by which a state carries out espionage might do so. Treaty law on the protection of human rights and intellectual property rights does not apply to extraterritorial acts of economic cyber espionage. States show no interest in negotiating new treaties on espionage, and state practice on spying shows no indication that new customary international law on espionage is forming.

---

[9]   China agreed that 'electronic intrusions' are prohibited acts for which natural and legal persons in China can be held legally liable by the Chinese government for engaging in trade secret misappropriation (art. 1.4(2) (a)). However, this provision does not address economic cyber espionage by or on behalf of the Chinese government against companies located in the United States. The United States did not claim the provision had such application.

5.3   Domestic law and cyber espionage

Countries use domestic law to authorize their governments to engage in espionage, regulate how their governments conduct espionage activities, and defend their governments and economies from spying conducted by other nations. However, the diversity in how countries use constitutional, statutory, and administrative law for intelligence and counterintelligence purposes, and how they conduct political and judicial oversight of these covert activities, makes it difficult to identify patterns across nations. The international efforts to harmonize domestic law on cybercrime (Section 3.3.3) have no equivalents in the areas of intelligence and counterintelligence. Espionage operations are shrouded in legally sanctioned secrecy, often making it impossible for the public to understand how governments interpret and apply domestic laws that authorize and regulate intelligence and counterintelligence activities. For example, Snowden's disclosures of US intelligence programmes generated controversies about the legitimacy in a democracy of a secret intelligence court issuing secret judgments based on secret interpretations of public laws.[10]

Even so, two patterns are discernible. First, the changing nature of national security threats encourages governments to increase their legal powers to conduct intelligence and counterintelligence. This pattern is apparent in how governments have sought additional authority to address the ways that criminals, terrorists, and spies threaten national security by exploiting the internet and digital technologies. Second, laws designed to defend against espionage, such as criminal prohibitions, do not deter foreign governments from spying, and this pattern prevails as well with cyber espionage (Section 5.3.2). The lack of deterrence by norms and by punishment means that countries create patchworks of legal measures to protect and defend against cyber espionage. The effectiveness of defensive measures is questionable. Government and private-sector information

---

[10]   Snowden's first disclosure was a secret order from the Foreign Intelligence Surveillance Court, which operates through classified proceedings, that required a telecommunication company to produce all telephony metadata it had for communications between the United States and foreign countries and for communications within the United States. The court based the order on an interpretation of the USA PATRIOT Act that was not publicly known.

systems are under relentless pressure because the offence has advantages over the defence in cyber espionage.

5.3.1   Conducting cyber espionage

Countries use domestic law to authorize and regulate the intelligence activities of their governments. The constitutional allocation of national security and foreign affairs powers often includes, or is interpreted to provide, legal authorization to conduct intelligence programmes. Legislation establishes and funds intelligence agencies and imposes limits on, and legislative and judicial oversight of, the actions of such agencies. Executive branch officials and intelligence agency officers issue directives and set policies that implement the legal authority provided by constitutional and statutory law. The extensive use of domestic law to authorize, support, and regulate intelligence activities demonstrates that states do not behave as if espionage is *per se* illegal under international law.

How states authorize and regulate intelligence agencies reflects many things, including how countries allocate government power through constitutional law, use legislation to balance competing interests and values against the need for foreign intelligence, and adjust interpretations of laws in response to changes in national security threats and technological innovation. These complex variables, differences in forms of government, diverse perspectives on national security threats, different levels of technological capabilities, and the secrecy that surrounds intelligence activities complicate identification of common characteristics in domestic legal systems on intelligence.

The emergence of cyber technologies, and public and private dependence on them, has stimulated increased government interest in expanded legal powers for intelligence, counterintelligence (Section 5.3.2), and law enforcement (Section 3.2.3). Changing perceptions of national security threats also contribute to government interest in broadening intelligence authorities and capabilities. In the cyber age, countries have encountered US hegemony in the post-Cold War period, global terrorism after 11 September 2001, and the return of balance-of-power politics with China's rise, Russia's assertiveness, and the perceived decline of the United States. The convergence of technological and geopolitical incentives to expand intelligence authorities and capabilities has produced concerns that more government power to conduct espionage threatens individual rights, economic activities, and international relations. Aided by disclosures of secret intelligence programmes, these concerns have prompted scrutiny of international law on espionage (Section 5.2.2) and domestic laws that govern intelligence activities, especially in democracies.

The re-examination of domestic law on intelligence activities in the United States after 11 September 2001 provides a high-profile example. The 11 September attacks were a catastrophic intelligence failure. In response, the legislative and executive branches expanded the intelligence community's legal authorities through, for example, the USA PATRIOT Act. Leaks to the press about US surveillance programmes, particularly Snowden's disclosures, triggered controversies about these authorities and how intelligence agencies interpreted and used them. These controversies encompassed constitutional law, including how intelligence agencies accessed and used the electronic communications of US nationals located outside the United States. New legislation, and revision of existing laws, attempted to achieve a new equilibrium between the government's interest in robust intelligence activities and the protection of the rights and liberties of Americans. The furore at home and abroad about US cyber espionage led the president to change policy on signals intelligence, including to direct the intelligence community to consider the privacy interests of foreign nationals in foreign countries in executing operations (Presidential Policy Directive/PPD-28 on Signals Intelligence (2014)).

Overall, this period witnessed one of the most comprehensive re-assessments of legal authorities on intelligence in US history. However, legal authorities for engaging in espionage against foreign countries and foreign nationals were not cut back. None of the US activities Snowden disclosed that constituted traditional espionage, such as gathering intelligence on foreign leaders or finding ways to counteract the encrypted communications of foreign intelligence services, violated US law. Policy changes within the executive branch focused on how the United States should exercise its legal authority rather than curtailing the scope of that authority. For example, the presidential directive that the intelligence community take the privacy interests of foreign nationals into account was a policy change not a reform mandated by constitutional law, legislation, or court decisions.

As seen in the USA FREEDOM Act (2015), legal reform focused instead on counterterrorism and counterintelligence operations (1) within the

United States; (2) affecting US nationals in the United States in communication with foreigners; and (3) US nationals residing in other countries. These reforms represented another attempt to strike the appropriate balance between US national security and individual liberty for Americans – a challenge other democratic nations face. Although the technologies implicated were new, the legal reforms focused on a traditional objective of US politics centred on the security of the republic and the freedom of its citizens.

Not every country that re-assessed the legal authorities for its intelligence agencies reached the same outcome. The German constitutional court ruled in 2020 that the privacy protections in Germany's constitution apply to German intelligence operations targeting foreign telecommunications. This decision changed what the German intelligence service could legally do in signals intelligence, including cyber espionage. The contrast between what happened in the United States and Germany underscores that national re-assessments of domestic legal authorities for intelligence operations often follow different paths.

However, evidence suggests that most countries have not taken the German approach. The rise of digital authoritarianism reflects how many governments are expanding their powers to conduct domestic surveillance. The increasing number of governments moving in this direction are unlikely to be, simultaneously, restricting their legal authority to engage in cyber espionage. The return of the balance of power also heightens incentives for states, especially the great powers, to maintain broad authority to engage in extensive cyber espionage in competing for influence in the international system. These observations are consistent with the conclusion that the controversies about cyber espionage did not change international law on espionage (Section 5.2).

5.3.2   Defending against cyber espionage

Protecting government information and criminalizing unauthorized access and use

Countries use domestic law to prevent foreign spies from gaining access to information of national security, foreign policy, or political importance. Governments restrict access to secret and sensitive government information to those persons authorized to use such information and to systems and places secured for accessing it. Governments treat unauthorized access and use of protected information as a criminal offence, regardless of the nationality of the offender. Typically, governments apply such criminal law to espionage that results in unauthorized access to, or use of, protected information. International law permits states to prescribe, but not enforce, such domestic criminal law extraterritorially (Section 3.3.1).

However, extraterritorial prescription of domestic criminal laws against espionage does not lead to prosecution and punishment of suspects located in foreign countries. Extradition treaties and MLATs (Section 3.3.2) are not useful when a country wants custody of, or information about activities undertaken by, a foreign government's spies. This problem arises when a country brings domestic charges against foreign government personnel for criminal offences related to cyber espionage. The US government has indicted persons working for foreign countries, such as China and Russia, for committing cyber espionage and cybercrime, but foreign governments do not extradite or cooperate, even if they have an extradition or mutual legal assistance treaty with the United States. Thus, domestic criminal laws have little, if any, deterrent effect against espionage, especially cyber espionage.

Protecting government information systems

As governments adopted computers and developed electronic information networks, efforts to restrict access to sensitive information expanded to include laws designed to secure government information systems from unauthorized access and use. Linking computers and networks through the internet increased the challenge, leading to the adoption of legal measures to strengthen the cybersecurity of government information systems. Such laws and measures do various things, such as assigning responsibility for cybersecurity to specific government actors; authorizing network defence operations (e.g., scanning for malware); creating oversight and accountability mechanisms; facilitating adoption of appropriate risk assessment and management practices; and mandating information sharing and reporting of breaches and other cybersecurity problems.

Even with such legal frameworks, achieving cybersecurity for government information systems has proved difficult, even for high-capability states. Despite efforts to improve the cybersecurity of its information systems, the US government has experienced many significant cyber-espionage breaches of its networks. Legal frameworks for government cybersecurity are necessary but not sufficient to defend government systems against cyber espionage. The problems confronting government cybersecurity underscore that, in cyberspace, the offence has the advantage over the defence. Efforts to defend government information systems do not produce deterrence by denial. Responses by governments that have systems breached (e.g., criminal charges against foreign spies) do not create deterrence by punishment – as evidenced by the uninterrupted efforts of intelligence agencies to penetrate the information systems of foreign governments. Countries are not interested in restraining espionage through international law (Section 5.2). As noted above, international cooperation on enforcing domestic criminal law on espionage is not effective. The only credible strategy against cyber espionage is building cyber defences for government information systems, but the advantages that foreign intelligence agencies have in conducting espionage puts this defensive strategy under constant pressure.

Counterintelligence operations

Governments also use law to support another defensive tactic – counterintelligence operations to identify, disrupt, and prevent espionage. Often, domestic counterintelligence operations must navigate more legal rules because constitutional and statutory law on protecting individual rights and regulating law-enforcement activities apply to these operations. Such rules might mean, for example, that domestic electronic surveillance against citizens, legal nationals, or foreign persons suspected of espionage faces more substantive limitations, procedural requirements, and political and judicial oversight than counterintelligence operations conducted extraterritorially against foreigners. In addition, domestic law might regulate extraterritorial counterintelligence operations that target citizens or nationals located in foreign countries.

As with law-enforcement efforts against cybercrime (Section 3.2) and counterterrorism activities on terrorist use of cyberspace (Sections 4.2 and 4.4), counterintelligence operations have generated friction between the government's interest in expanded surveillance powers and opposition to surveillance that threatens civil and political rights protected by domestic law. Although counterterrorism was the most prominent justification, the surveillance programmes disclosed by Snowden, including the bulk collection of electronic communications, also served counterintelligence purposes. Searching databases of electronic communications collected in bulk could help counterintelligence agencies identify whether someone within a nation's territory was communicating with agents of a foreign government. Such information could then support targeted surveillance of that person's activities to prevent or disrupt espionage and punish spies. Thus, legal and policy changes made to surveillance programmes in response to Snowden-related controversies affected counterintelligence as well as counterterrorism.

However, the impact of expanded legal authorities for surveillance on counterintelligence efforts against cyber espionage is not clear. Foreign governments engaged in cyber espionage often have more resources, expertise, and technologies than criminals or terrorists, which makes the counterintelligence challenge posed by cyber espionage more difficult. Continued revelations about damaging breaches of government information systems by cyber espionage are evidence of failures of cybersecurity and counterintelligence. The significant infiltration of US government information systems revealed at the end of 2020 went undetected for a long time. A cybersecurity company identified this cyber espionage campaign before any US counterintelligence agency did. Such failures of counterintelligence highlight, again, the advantages that the offence has over the defence in the cyber realm. In addition, as in the law-enforcement and counterterrorism contexts, encrypted communications present counterintelligence agencies with challenges in dealing with cyber espionage. Even so, given the long relationship between encryption and spy craft, counterintelligence agencies have more experience countering espionage conducted through encrypted communications.

Defending against economic cyber espionage

Countries attempt to defend private-sector enterprises that develop and use intellectual property and trade secrets against economic cyber espionage conducted by foreign governments or their proxies. Some governments use non-state actors, such as cybercriminals, to conduct economic cyber espionage. International law does not prohibit this practice because espionage does not violate international law (Section 5.2). Governments criminalize economic espionage; but, as with traditional espionage, domestic criminal law is not effective, especially against economic cyber espionage. Efforts by governments to bring foreigners accused of economic cyber espionage to justice usually fail because international law-enforcement cooperation, such as through extradition and MLATs, does not work for this problem.

However, defending against economic cyber espionage proves more legally complicated than defending governments against cyber espionage. Companies, not government agencies, control the information systems infiltrated by foreign governments seeking commercial information. In many countries, this fact replays the controversies over whether and how governments should regulate the cybersecurity practices of privately owned and operated critical infrastructure (Section 4.3) and companies that sell national security goods and services to governments. Economic cyber espionage affects the private sector well beyond critical infrastructure and defence contractors. Defending companies against such espionage has the same scope as protecting the private sector against cybercrime – a sobering analogy given the growing scale of cybercrime and the ineffectiveness of measures adopted to combat it (Chapter 3).

Governments have used law to authorize government agencies to share information with the private sector and ensure that companies are legally protected when they share cybersecurity information with the government. The strategy is to improve situational awareness about what governments and companies encounter in defending information networks. Better situational awareness can help governments and companies identify and act against economic cyber espionage faster, potentially mitigating the damage it inflicts on corporate enterprises and national economies. Strengthened public-private information sharing can create trust and incentives for bolstering private-sector cyber defences, such as cooperation on frameworks to guide corporate assessment and management of cybersecurity risks.

Some governments have gone beyond information-sharing programmes to mandate that companies take certain actions to improve cybersecurity.[11] Such mandates could be procedural, such as requirements to conduct cybersecurity audits of corporate systems and report to shareholders or governments certain information about cybersecurity actions taken and incidents experienced. Mandates can also be substantive in requiring, for example, the use of technologies (e.g., certified software), techniques (e.g.,

---

[11]   See the discussion of cybersecurity mandates on companies that operate critical infrastructure in Section 4.3.1.

cloud services), and tools (e.g., encryption) that can improve cybersecurity cost-effectively.

A mixture of procedural and substantive mandates appears in the EU's proposal for a binding directive on cybersecurity that would apply to private-sector enterprises beyond critical infrastructure providers. The proposed directive would impose a risk management approach that requires implementation of basic cybersecurity policies and practices.[12] This directive, and similar legal strategies by other countries, is not designed to defend only against economic cyber espionage. Rather, such mandates support private-sector development of 'all hazards' defences against cyber threats from cybercriminals, terrorists, and spies. Whether more robust use of mandates on the private sector produces better defences against economic cyber espionage remains to be seen. Governments keen to engage in economic cyber espionage will not be deterred by increased regulation of private-sector cybersecurity. For years to come, intelligence agencies will have a target-rich environment unevenly defended because countries will adopt fragmented approaches, and many companies will not have adequate capabilities to protect themselves from foreign cyber spies.

5.3.3   Balancing cyber offence and defence: The zero-day vulnerability problem

Countries have incentives to conduct cyber espionage and defend against it, but these incentives are in tension concerning how governments manage 'zero-day vulnerabilities' – software flaws not previously identified that might create opportunities for gaining unauthorized access to information networks. For intelligence agencies, such vulnerabilities can be valuable for conducting cyber espionage. Intelligence agencies hunt for zero-day bugs, as well as buy them from hackers. However, zero-day vulnerabilities only have offensive value if they remain secret. Disclosing them to software companies and users usually leads to patches and other fixes that improve cyber defences in the public and private sectors. The tension between keeping zero-day vulnerabilities secret or disclosing them also appears with law-enforcement surveillance against criminal activities (Chapter 3) and military use of cyber weapons (Chapter 6).

---

12   European Commission, *Proposal for a Directive on Measures for High Common Level of Cybersecurity across the Union*, 16 December 2020.

The need to weigh the offensive potential of secret zero-day vulnerabilities against the defensive value of disclosing them has led several countries to develop a 'vulnerabilities equities process' (VEP). Generally, under this process, a government gathers input from agencies dealing with military, intelligence, law enforcement, cybersecurity, and commercial issues to identify the risks and benefits of disclosing zero-day vulnerabilities or keeping them secret. The VEP evaluates those risks and benefits in balancing the offensive and defensive interests – or equities – concerning how to handle software flaws. The process makes a recommendation or decision about whether to disclose vulnerabilities or keep them secret. Not every country has a VEP, and not every government with one acknowledges its existence or discusses how it works. For countries that have them, VEPs do not operate or balance the equities identically because governments differ in how they manage cybersecurity threats, conduct interagency consultations, value transparency in national security policy, and evaluate the risks and benefits of disclosing zero-day vulnerabilities.

The existence and importance of VEPs first emerged in the United States. Snowden's leaks in 2013 included examples of the National Security Agency's exploitation of zero-day vulnerabilities. These disclosures generated controversy about how much the US government was hiding and hoarding zero-day bugs. In response, the Obama administration shared some information about the US VEP, which generated more questions and debate. The US government took additional steps to make its VEP more transparent. In 2017, the Trump administration released the Vulnerabilities Equities Policy and Process for the United States Government. This 'VEP Charter' described how the US government would protect 'core internet infrastructure, information systems, critical infrastructure systems, and the US economy through disclosure of vulnerabilities … absent a demonstrable, overriding interest in the use of the vulnerability for lawful intelligence, law enforcement, or national security purposes'.

The US debate about zero-day vulnerabilities led other countries to address the issue. In 2017, Canada acknowledged that it had a VEP. In 2018, the UK government described the process and decision criteria it uses in determining whether to disclose software vulnerabilities or retain them for law enforcement, intelligence, or other national security reasons. Also in 2018, Germany indicated that it needed a VEP as part of its evolving cybersecurity policies. These developments informed efforts to understand and make more transparent how other states, such as other EU members and India, handled zero-day vulnerabilities. These activities stimulated the Transatlantic Cyber Forum to propose a model process for government decisions on whether to disclose vulnerabilities or keep them secret.[13]

Although VEPs have become a major cybersecurity issue, this prominence does not mean that states have developed much domestic and international law on zero-day vulnerabilities. In terms of domestic law, VEPs that have been described, such as the VEP Charter in the United States, appear to be policy frameworks based on general national security authority rather than directives issued under legislation specifically on government handling of zero-day vulnerabilities. Advocates for making VEPs more transparent, balanced, and effective often argue for the adoption of laws to regulate how governments assess and manage zero-day vulnerabilities. The Transatlantic Cyber Forum's model policy process contains the principle that a VEP 'needs to be enshrined in law, with an independent legislative review of its effectiveness and proportionality, or a sunset clause, after five (5) years'.

Turning to international law, countries have adopted no treaties on zero-day vulnerabilities. Customary international law has not formed because state practice on disclosure of such vulnerabilities is not general, consistent, or supported by a sense of legal obligation. Debates and developments concerning VEPs are concentrated in democratic states, and not much is known about how China, Russia, and other non-democratic countries manage zero-day vulnerabilities. In addition, questions remain about how VEPs adopted by countries operate in balancing the offensive and defensive equities of software flaws, which further complicates identifying common approaches across nations on government handling of zero-day vulnerabilities.

---

[13] Sven Herpig, *Governmental Vulnerability Assessment and Management – Weighing Temporary Retention versus Immediate Disclosure of 0-Day Vulnerabilities: A Proposal Supported by the Transatlantic Cyber Forum* (Stiftung Neue Verantwortung, August 2018).

5.4   Beyond cyber espionage: Covert cyber operations

In addition to espionage and counterintelligence, states use intelligence agencies for clandestine activities that attempt to influence events in other nations. Such covert operations or actions can involve spreading propaganda to affect elections, interfering with economic activities, assassinating individuals, sabotaging critical infrastructure, or supporting insurgents in overthrowing governments. Unlike espionage, states have historically considered many types of covert operations to violate international law under the rules on sovereignty, non-intervention, and the prohibition on the use of force. However, a presumption of illegality has not stopped states from engaging in covert operations. The perceived utility of covert action, and the potential for it to cause national and international political and legal problems for a government, has meant some countries attempt to regulate this activity under domestic law.

Governments have tapped cyber technologies to conduct covert operations. Cyberspace creates heightened incentives to engage in covert action because cyber technologies provide new capabilities – including ways to make attribution difficult – and internet dependence produces more exploitable vulnerabilities. Many types of cyber incidents can best be interpreted as covert actions, including:

- Hacking to obtain private or protected information and releasing the information to damage individuals, officials, corporations, or governments (e.g., Russia's 'hack-and-leak' operation during the US elections in 2016);
- Disseminating disinformation online to influence domestic politics, including elections, in other countries (e.g., disinformation campaigns on social media by various countries during US elections in 2016, 2018, and 2020);
- Using distributed denial of service (DDoS) attacks and similar techniques to disrupt information and communication systems (e.g., the Chinese DDoS attack in 2019 against Hong Kong residents participating in protests);
- Planting malware in an adversary's information systems for later use, such as during a crisis (e.g., the 'logic bomb' that North Korea planted in 2013 against South Korean financial institutions); and

- Disrupting, manipulating, and damaging software, data, computers, networks, or computer-operated machinery (e.g., the Stuxnet attack exposed in 2010 by the United States and Israel that destroyed centrifuges in an Iranian uranium-enrichment facility).

The range of potential covert cyber operations produces challenges for international law.[14] The *Tallinn Manual 2.0* concluded that disinformation campaigns do not violate the rules on sovereignty and non-intervention (318–19).[15] Even though it constituted foreign meddling in the democratic process, the United States did not argue that the Russian hack-and-leak operation during its elections in 2016 violated the rules on sovereignty and non-intervention. A covert cyber operation that damages or destroys its targets constitutes an illegal use of force and, depending on its severity, potentially an armed attack triggering the victim's right to use force in self-defence (Sections 6.3.1 and 6.3.2). The international lawyers crafting the *Tallinn Manual 2.0* agreed that the Stuxnet operation, which destroyed hundreds of uranium-enrichment centrifuges, constituted an illegal use of force, but they could not agree on whether the effects were serious enough to make it an armed attack (*Tallinn Manual 2.0*, 342). Between disinformation campaigns and cyber sabotage are a host of possible covert cyber operations that states can execute and, in the process, exploit controversies about when states violate sovereignty, illegally intervene in another state's domestic affairs, engage in a prohibited use of force, or commit an illegal armed attack. In short, international law does little, if anything, to shrink the incentives that states have for engaging in covert cyber operations.

The attractiveness of covert cyber operations raises questions about how states use domestic law to regulate covert action. In many countries, domestic regulation of covert operations emerged before cyber technologies in response to perceived government abuses of the power to engage in covert action. By and large, these pre-cyber regulations apply to covert cyber operations. Finding patterns in the regulation of covert action across countries is difficult given differences in constitutional allocations of power, diversity in legal systems, and the heightened secrecy that sur-

---

[14] See also the discussion on cyber operations not constituting uses of force in Section 6.3.9.

[15] On non-intervention and cyber operations, see Ido Kilovaty, 'The International Law of Cyber Intervention', in *Research Handbook on International Law and Cyberspace*, 97–112.

rounds this clandestine area. Generally, states have used domestic law to (1) define what constitutes covert action by, for example, distinguishing covert action from military operations; (2) ban certain activities, such as assassinating foreign officials; and (3) achieve more transparency and accountability for covert actions by imposing documentation, reporting, funding, and oversight requirements. As with cyber espionage, domestic law applicable to foreign covert cyber operations, such as criminal laws against unauthorized access to and manipulation of information systems, does not deter foreign governments from engaging in covert cyber action.

The threat of covert cyber action underscores the need for better cyber defences. The scale of the defensive task, and past failures to strengthen public and private-sector cyber defences, has stimulated interest in deterring covert cyber actions through threats of cyber retaliation. As in other areas of cybersecurity, whether deterrence by punishment works against covert cyber action remains unclear. The United States launched a covert cyber operation that temporarily disabled some of Russia's capabilities to conduct information operations during the US election in 2018. Some hailed this operation as an example of effective deterrence, but the operation attempted to prevent, rather than deter, Russian interference in the election. The perceived success of the operation reinforced the attractiveness of covert cyber operations for states and the importance for governments to develop the capabilities to engage in them.

6　Cyber war

In cybersecurity, 'cyber war' is a misused concept. Almost every type of cyber incident has been called an act of war or cited as evidence that cyber war is underway. However, war does not encompass all malign behaviour by state and non-state actors. Armed conflict involves the use of force that produces damage or destruction to property, and injury or death to persons, on a scale that requires specific treatment in policy and law. Whether a kinetic or cyber event crosses this threshold sometimes proves difficult to determine. Nevertheless, countries distinguish armed conflict from crime, terrorism, and espionage in determining how to respond to cyber threats.

This chapter covers the relationship between cyber technologies and armed conflict. After looking at the cyber war problem (Section 6.1), the chapter explores domestic and international legal issues concerning the decision to engage in armed conflict (Sections 6.2 and 6.3). These rules developed before cyber technologies emerged. Understanding whether such technologies affect how countries use these rules is important. The capabilities that cyber technologies provide have also forced countries to respond to hostile cyber incidents that do not constitute armed conflict. The chapter then considers how international humanitarian law – also called the law of armed conflict – applies to cyber operations in armed conflict (Section 6.4). This topic has been extensively studied.[1] However,

---

[1]   The NATO Cooperative Cyber Defence Centre of Excellence sponsored the *Tallinn Manual on the International Law Applicable to Cyber Warfare* (Michael N. Schmitt, gen. ed.) (CUP, 2013) and the *Tallinn Manual 2.0 on the International Law Applicable to Cyber Operations* (Michael N. Schmitt, gen. ed.) (CUP, 2nd edn, 2017) [hereinafter *Tallinn Manual 2.0*], which analyse how international humanitarian law (IHL) applies to cyber operations. For the rest of this chapter, references to the *Tallinn Manual 2.0* appear in the main text. The ICRC, a non-governmental organization focused on IHL, has addressed cyber operations in armed conflict.

the few known cases of cyber operations in armed conflict have been difficult to interpret given a lack of information about them and their consequences. The chapter concludes with a look at whether arms control and related strategies, such as confidence-building measures, are relevant to cyber technologies (Section 6.5).

6.1 The cyber war problem

The relationship between cyber technologies and armed conflict has produced three general perspectives:

- Cyber technologies permit hostile activities among states of a type, and on a scale and intensity, that challenges conventional concepts of armed conflict. Applying traditional notions of war to cyber technologies minimizes the nature and danger of cyber threats and constrains potential responses to cyber hostility, such as deterrence by punishment.
- Governments can start a war, in the traditional sense, through cyber operations (e.g., US fears about a 'cyber Pearl Harbor' attack). Militaries can also use kinetic and cyber weapons synergistically in warfare. The ways that cyber technologies slot into traditional conceptions of armed conflict makes understanding how domestic and international law apply to cyber operations imperative to inform how governments develop and use military cyber capabilities.
- Cyber technologies represent a new, full-spectrum capability that requires integration into all military functions, strategy, doctrine, tactics, and rules of engagement. The challenge for militaries goes beyond compliance with the law on entering, and engaging in, armed conflict and includes how militaries conduct cyber espionage, undertake covert cyber action, strengthen cyber defence, and create cyber deterrence.

Although distinct, these perspectives are not mutually exclusive, and how they overlap helps explain the approaches many countries have taken. The differences between cyber and kinetic weapons create opportunities

---

See ICRC, *International Humanitarian Law and Cyber Operations during Armed Conflicts: ICRC Position Paper* (November 2019).

for governments to exploit cyber technologies outside armed conflict in hostile activities that do not qualify as uses of force (Section 6.3.9). Many countries prefer keeping the legal thresholds for what constitutes armed force and armed conflict set in the pre-cyber era rather than changing the rules because cyber is different. In addition, cyber operations are attractive under international humanitarian law because they offer less destructive and less lethal capabilities than kinetic weapons. Here, too, the fact that cyber is different reinforces commitment to existing rules rather than generating demand for change. Thus, many states have emphasized developing cyber capabilities and integrating them into military command-and-control structures, strategy, doctrine, tactics, and training. This pattern suggests governments believe that armed conflict in the future will involve coordinated kinetic and cyber operations rather than war conducted only in cyberspace.

Efforts by the United States to develop and integrate cyber capabilities into military operations illustrate the incentives and pattern described above. The United States created a unified combatant command – US Cyber Command – to direct, synchronize, and coordinate military cyber operations. The US government has developed military cyber strategies; issued directives to guide military cyber operations; addressed cyber operations in its application of the law of armed conflict; passed legislation authorizing the military to conduct specific offensive cyber operations; coordinated with civilian agencies on strengthening cyber defences; and conducted offensive military cyber operations during and outside of armed conflict. These activities, and similar ones by other governments, underscore how countries are mainstreaming cyber capabilities into military forces and operations as another instrument of national power.

The development of military cyber capabilities has not been without controversy. The creation and strengthening of such capabilities have produced fears about the 'militarization' of cyberspace and cybersecurity through military involvement in civilian cyber defence, law-enforcement, intelligence and counterintelligence, covert actions, and incident response and recovery efforts. In many countries, military cyber forces are better funded and staffed than the cyber capabilities that civilian government agencies, critical infrastructure operators, and private-sector enterprises have. Expanding the military's involvement in whole-of-government and whole-of-society approaches to improving cybersecurity often proves tempting.

A debate has also emerged over what role military cyber capabilities play in cyber deterrence. The intensity of cybercrime and cyber espionage demonstrates that military cyber forces do not deter these threats, and, historically, governments have not embraced deterrence by punishment as a strategy against cybercrime or cyber espionage (Sections 3.2.5 and 5.1). The military cyber power that countries are building does not explain the lack of terrorist cyberattacks (Chapter 4). Some countries have used military cyber capabilities to launch covert actions to prevent or disrupt – rather than deter – hostile cyber operations, such as disinformation campaigns, and military cyber capabilities have increased rather than dampened government interest in covert operations (Section 5.4). The development of military cyber capabilities also does not explain the absence of large-scale, destructive, and lethal cyberattacks launched outside of armed conflict. Incentives to engage in such a military cyberattack are weak for many reasons, including that it would trigger kinetic warfare between the victim and the aggressor.

Despite little evidence that military cyber capabilities deter hostile cyber operations, cybersecurity debates often involve proposals to use military cyber power to retaliate against foreign state and non-state actors to deter such operations. Escalating ransomware attacks by cybercriminals has prompted arguments that the United States should go on the cyber offensive against them (Section 3.3.4), with the US military's cyber campaign against the Islamic State during an armed conflict with that terrorist group (Section 6.4.4) offered as a precedent.[2]

Advocacy for using military cyber capabilities against foreign cybercriminal operations exposes several problems in cybersecurity policy, including the weaknesses of the law-enforcement approach to cybercrime (Sections 3.2 and 3.3), the inadequacy of domestic cyber defences (Sections 3.2.5 and 3.3.4), the willingness of some countries to provide havens for cybercriminals (Section 3.3.4), and the temptation to use military capabilities to address cybersecurity threats outside of armed conflict. In addition, this option is only available to a few states that have the requisite cyber capabilities to conduct offensive cyber operations and sufficient power in the international system to cope with the consequences of launching such operations.

---

[2]   Dmitri Alperovitch, 'America is Being Held for Ransom. It Needs to Fight Back', *New York Times*, 20 September 2021.

How military capabilities relate to civilian cyber defence has also produced controversies. For countries that draw lines between civilian and military authority, involving the military in strengthening civilian cyber defences raises issues that governments must manage to maintain civilian and military spheres of activity and civilian control of the military. As happens with intelligence activities and covert actions, incentives not to disclose zero-day vulnerabilities because they are useful for military cyber operations are in tension with civilian efforts to reduce risks associated with unpatched software (Section 5.3.3). Military cyber operations – and the theft of cyber weapons – can make means and methods of conducting cyber hostilities available to criminals, terrorists, and foreign states in ways that threaten the cyber defences of civilian government agencies, critical infrastructure operators, and the private sector.[3]

The rest of this chapter focuses on cyber technologies and armed conflict. However, the militarization of cybersecurity policy, the questionable contribution of military cyber power to cyber deterrence, and the problems that military activities can cause for civilian cyber defence demonstrate that military cyber capabilities create cybersecurity challenges beyond armed conflict.

6.2   Going to war in cyberspace: Domestic law and war powers

Domestic and international law play important roles when governments decide whether to go to war. The rules developed in the pre-cyber world, so the law does not reflect issues that cyber technologies uniquely create. Government decisions to enter armed conflict will hinge on more than what militaries can do with cyber technologies. The armed conflict between Georgia and Russia that began in 2008 featured DDoS attacks (Section 6.4.3), but both countries went to war for reasons having nothing

---

[3]   Offensive cyber operations expose the techniques used, such as whether zero-day vulnerabilities were exploited. This exposure creates opportunities for other actors to copy or modify those techniques in, for example, cyber-crime and cyber espionage. Arsenals of cyber weapons are also vulnerable to theft, as seen when cyber weapons developed by the US National Security Agency were stolen and then used by China, North Korea, and Russia.

to do with cyberspace. Several nations engaged in armed conflict with the Islamic State starting in 2014 before coalition militaries launched cyber operations against that terrorist group (Section 6.4.4). Countries that engage in armed conflict likely will do so with more than cyber weapons, which means the decision to enter armed conflict will depend on more than cyber considerations. Even so, governments could use cyber weapons in ways that trigger armed conflict.

6.2.1 Stuxnet as a case study

The cyber incident that has drawn the most attention for approaching the line between peace and war is the Stuxnet operation exposed in 2010 that Israel and the United States conducted against Iran. Neither Israel nor the United States acknowledged its role, but the evidence that they executed the attack is persuasive. Stuxnet was a computer worm that targeted industrial control systems at Iranian uranium-enrichment centrifuge facilities. Stuxnet re-programmed the systems and made the centrifuges spin at high speeds to damage them. Stuxnet further manipulated the systems to have the centrifuges report normal functioning. This operation involved extensive intelligence work, use of zero-day vulnerabilities, anti-virus evasion tactics, network infection abilities, and injection of updates. The Stuxnet attack resulted in physical damage to, or destruction of, hundreds of centrifuges in Iran.

The operation's sophistication was clear, but questions arose about what Stuxnet constituted in legal terms. The attack involved criminal activities, such as gaining unauthorized access to computers, but cybercrime did not define this operation in policy or legal terms. Stuxnet was never considered cyber terrorism because only highly capable states could have undertaken it, and Israel and the United States were identified as the perpetrators. Stuxnet involved cyber espionage, but the operation went beyond spying to involve covert cyber sabotage. Experts debated whether Stuxnet constituted an illegal use of force, armed attack, and act of aggression. Sections 6.2 and 6.3 use Stuxnet as a case study to illuminate the issues that arise under domestic and international law concerning when countries decide to engage in armed conflict.

6.2.2   War powers in domestic law

Domestic law regulates how a government exercises its war powers – the legal authority to order military forces to engage in armed conflict. How constitutional and statutory law govern the exercise of this authority differs among countries. For example, constitutional law in Germany and Japan places more constraints on the deployment and use of military forces than the constitutions of other countries. Generally, domestic law:

- Allocates authority among the branches of government for the exercise of control over a nation's military forces, such as the legislature's primacy in funding the military and the executive branch's role in commanding military forces;
- Identifies when the government can use military force, such as in response to an invasion, an armed attack on the country or its military forces, or an armed attack on a treaty ally; and
- Assigns authority for determining when the criteria for using military force are met, such as requiring legislative authorization before deployment of military forces into combat.

International law also informs decisions whether to use military force (Section 6.3), but a decision to engage in armed conflict through a declaration of war, or an authorization to use military force, can comply with domestic law while violating international law. In 2003, the US Congress and the UK government exercised their respective constitutional powers by authorizing the use of military force against Iraq, but controversy raged whether international law provided any justification for the invasion of Iraq.

Under domestic law, decisions to authorize military force do not typically specify what weapons the military can use. Countries restrict or prohibit the development and use of certain weapons (Section 6.5), but such measures operate independent of decisions to use military force. An authorization under domestic law to use military force usually encompasses all military capabilities that a country can legally deploy in armed conflict. The military chain of command determines which means and methods to use based on the strategy, tactics, and capabilities needed to defeat the adversary in compliance with international humanitarian law (Section 6.4).

In some countries, controversies have arisen over the legal authority to undertake military operations in situations not recognized in domestic law as bases for using force, such as humanitarian interventions to prevent or stop genocide. In the UK, the authority to use military force was traditionally considered a prerogative power of the government in which Parliament had no legal role. However, parliamentary debates and votes on the deployment of UK military forces in the past two decades produced a war powers 'convention' that recognizes some role for Parliament in decisions to authorize the use of military force. US presidents have maintained that they have constitutional power to use military force in limited ways without legislative authorization in contexts that do not involve armed attacks against the United States, its military, or its treaty allies. The exercise of this authority has provoked controversies about the constitutional allocation of war powers that legislation, namely the War Powers Resolution (1973), and lawsuits have not resolved.

For countries that experience disagreements about war powers in domestic law, cyber weapons do not transform the debate. Legal controversies concerning war powers have arisen in connection with claims of authority to engage in kinetic military operations. The use of cyber capabilities in large or limited military engagements does not expand the scope of the authority already claimed to undertake lethal, destructive military operations. For example, without congressional authorization, President Barack Obama engaged the United States in a NATO air campaign against the Libyan government in 2011 to support humanitarian intervention. The UK government authorized the UK military's participation in this intervention without a debate or vote in Parliament. The United States and the UK dropped thousands of kinetic munitions on targets in Libya. The UK government's authorization of military force would have included cyber operations had the British military conducted any. President Obama considered, but rejected, launching cyberattacks to disable Libyan air defences. The claimed presidential authority to launch kinetic operations on the scale undertaken by the United States would have covered less lethal and destructive cyberattacks. The constitutional power permitting the US president to engage in limited military operations could also authorize a decision to use cyber weapons rather than conventional munitions. This presidential authority could have justified US participation in the Stuxnet attack. In the event, the US government categorized Stuxnet as a covert action by its intelligence agencies (Section 5.4) rather than as a military activity.

However, the development of military cyber capabilities raises the concern that such capabilities might provide governments with more incentive to engage in limited military operations under claimed legal authority to do so. In the UK, efforts to clarify when Parliament has a role in decisions to use military force have taken note of the challenges that military cyber capabilities present to identifying when parliamentary involvement should happen. To date, publicly available information suggests this scenario has not played out in the United States. Congress has authorized military cyber operations acknowledged by the US government, such as the disruption of Russian information operations targeting the 2018 US elections, or that came in response to an attack on US military forces, such as the cyberattack against Iran in response to its downing of a US military drone in 2019.

Domestic laws also establish oversight processes, such as requirements for defence agencies to provide information to legislative bodies, that apply to military cyber operations. US law mandates that the Secretary of Defense brief congressional committees 'about any military activities or operations in cyberspace, including clandestine military activities or operations in cyberspace' (10 USC, sec. 394(d)). Such reporting requirements allow the legislature to understand how military forces are being used, what weapons are being deployed, and whether military activities comply with the law. Legislative review often does not focus on whether the use of military forces was legally authorized, but such oversight can address this issue. Courts can also exercise oversight over military activities; but, in many countries, courts are reluctant to resolve disputes between the legislative and executive branches over war powers or interfere with military strategy and tactics, including choice of weapons.

6.3 Going to war in cyberspace: International law on the use of force

6.3.1 The prohibition of the use of force and the right to use force in self-defence

International law prohibits the threat or use of force by states (UN Charter, art. 2(4)). The only universally recognized exceptions to this prohibition are when a state uses force (1) under a UN Security Council decision authorizing the use of force in response to a threat to international peace and security; and (2) in response to an armed attack under its inherent right of self-defence (UN Charter, arts 39, 42, and 51). The prohibition of the use or threat of force applies to cyber technologies, but how it applies has generated questions because a technology unlike previous weaponry is being evaluated under rules that have long been controversial.[4]

Despite being a fundamental rule of international law, the prohibition of the use of force has caused contentious debate for decades. The same is true for controversies concerning the right to use force in self-defence and for humanitarian intervention. In this difficult context, the range of consequences that cyber weapons can produce creates challenges for legal analysis. In addition, very few, if any, cyber incidents have involved a use of force or constituted an armed attack, so little state practice exists on applying the prohibition, and its exceptions, to cyber operations. To date, the cyber incident that has garnered the most attention under these rules is Stuxnet.

According to the *Tallinn Manual 2.0*, a 'cyber operation that constitutes a threat or use of force against the territorial integrity or political independence of any State, or that is in any other manner inconsistent with the purposes of the United Nations, is unlawful' (Rule 68).[5] A state may use force in self-defence if it experiences 'a cyber operation that rises to the level of an armed attack' (*Tallinn Manual 2.0*, Rule 71).[6] These rules highlight that international law on the use of force contains two thresholds that identify what rules apply (Figure 6.1) The use-of-force threshold signals when state action becomes a use of force. The armed-attack threshold marks when the scale and severity of a use of force trigger a victim state's right to use force in self-defence.

---

[4]   See, e.g., Marco Roscini, 'Cyber Operations as a Use of Force', in Nicholas Tsagourias and Russell Buchan, eds, *Research Handbook on International Law and Cyberspace* (Edward Elgar, 2nd edn, 2021) [hereinafter *Research Handbook on International Law and Cyberspace*], 296–315.

[5]   The *Tallinn Manuals* are not official documents produced by intergovernmental negotiations. The NATO Cooperative Cyber Defence Centre of Excellence convened an International Group of Experts to capture what the experts considered to be the state of international law on cyber operations. Although without legal status, the manuals are authoritative contributions to understanding how international law applies to cyber operations. Work on the *Tallinn Manual 3.0* is underway.

[6]   See, e.g., Carlo Focarelli, 'Self-Defence in Cyberspace', in *Research Handbook on International Law and Cyberspace*, 316–43.

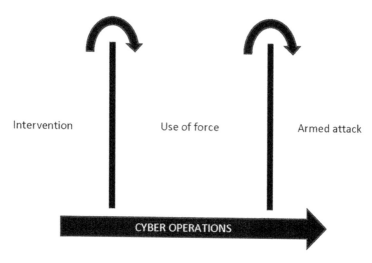

Figure 6.1   The use-of-force and armed-attack thresholds in international law

6.3.2   Determining what is a 'use of force' and an 'armed attack'

Despite the importance of these thresholds, international law does not define 'use of force' or 'armed attack'. In deciding whether actions constitute a use of force or armed attack, states analyse the character, context, and consequences of the actions in question on a case-by-case basis. In this assessment, the nature, scale, and severity of the actual and foreseeable consequences are the most important criteria. To be a use of force, a cyber operation's scale and effects must be 'comparable to non-cyber operations rising to the level of a use of force' (*Tallinn Manual 2.0*, Rule 69). Cyber operations 'that injure or kill persons or physically damage or destroy objects are uses of force' (*Tallinn Manual 2.0*, 333). To be an armed attack, a cyber operation's scale and effects must be greater and more severe than a use of force. A cyber operation crosses that threshold when it 'seriously injures or kills a number of persons or … causes significant damage to, or destruction of, property' (*Tallinn Manual 2.0*, 341).

The *Tallinn Manual 2.0* applied this scale-and-effects approach to Stuxnet. The International Group of Experts concluded that the operation constituted a use of force because it damaged or destroyed property. The group did not reach agreement on whether the damage was severe enough for Stuxnet to be an armed attack. However, when the world learned about Stuxnet, the reactions of states did not reflect consensus that Stuxnet was a use of force. Post-Stuxnet state practice suggested that, perhaps, governments evaluate damage or destruction caused by cyber operations differently than damage or destruction caused by kinetic weapons. Put another way, where states draw the use-of-force and armed-attack thresholds for cyber operations might diverge from how states evaluate consequences associated with kinetic weapons.[7]

This conjecture remains speculation because Stuxnet remains the only known incident that has seriously tested whether a cyber operation crossed the use-of-force and armed-attack thresholds. Other than Stuxnet, the *Tallinn Manual 2.0* identified no other cyber operation that constituted a use of force or generated serious debate about whether it was an armed attack. Since the manual's publication in 2017, no other publicly disclosed or exposed cyber operation has produced agreement among governments and cyber experts that it constituted a use of force or armed attack. Many possible cyber operations could qualify as a use of force or armed attack, including operations that cause airplanes to crash, nuclear power plants to meltdown and release harmful radiation, and dams to malfunction and flood populated regions. However, post-Stuxnet cyber operations have not pushed up against the use-of-force and armed-attack thresholds.

The lack of cyber incidents that cross the use-of-force threshold raises the question whether the prohibition on the use of force effectively regulates cyber operations by states, creating deterrence by norms. States planning or experiencing cyber operations will consider 'the international community's probable assessment of whether the operations violate the prohibition of the use of force' (*Tallinn Manual 2.0*, 333). Equally plausible is that states believe cyber operations less harmful than Stuxnet-type actions advance their interests more effectively. The pattern of states conducting many cyber operations below the use-of-force threshold likely results from the convergence of political preference and norm deterrence.

---

[7]   Interestingly, Iran's statement about how international law applies in cyberspace 'appears to set a high threshold' for when a cyber operation would qualify as a use of force. Michael N. Schmitt, 'Noteworthy Releases of International Cyber Law Positions – Part II: Iran', *Articles of War*, 27 August 2020.

6.3.3 Responding to a use of force or an armed attack

If a state is the victim of a use of force, then it can respond with peaceful countermeasures (e.g., economic sanctions) proportionate to the injury incurred (*Tallinn Manual 2.0*, Rules 20 and 23).[8] Countermeasures responding to a cyber use of force are not restricted to the cyber realm, but cyber countermeasures to a cyber use of force do not mean the countermeasures are, by definition, proportionate. A state can resort to necessary and proportionate force in self-defence in the immediate aftermath of an armed attack (*Tallinn Manual 2.0*, Rules 71–3) (see also Section 6.3.4 on anticipatory self-defence).[9] A state can use kinetic force in response to a cyber armed attack, if that use of force is necessary and proportionate. A cyber use of force in response to a cyber armed attack does not, by itself, constitute necessary and proportionate force under the right to use force in self-defence.

Cyber capabilities provide governments with attractive options for proportionate countermeasures and for using force in self-defence. After an Iranian surface-to-air missile shot down a US surveillance drone in 2019, the United States conducted cyber operations against Iranian missile control facilities and an Iranian military database allegedly used in executing attacks on oil tankers in the Persian Gulf. President Donald Trump opted for the cyber operations after determining that US missile strikes would have been a disproportionate response. Iran and the United States disagreed about the facts of the incident – whether the drone was in Iranian or international airspace – and how international law applied to it – whether the downing of the drone was an armed attack or just a use of force. Whether the US cyber operations crossed the use-of-force threshold remained ambiguous given the lack of information about what consequences the operations produced. Even so, the ability to conduct

---

8 Countermeasures are acts that violate international law but are permitted as responses to prior violations to bring the state committing the initial violation back into compliance with international law. States can also respond to violations of international law through retorsion, unfriendly acts that do not violate international law.

9 Countries recognized the 11 September 2001 terrorist attacks as an armed attack triggering the right of the United States to use force in self-defence. Although fears of a 'cyber 9/11' exist, terrorists have exhibited no capability to conduct cyber operations that could injure, kill, damage, and destroy on the scale of the 11 September attacks (Chapter 4).

cyber operations facilitated a more proportionate response than kinetic missile strikes and helped de-escalate a situation that had the two countries on the brink of more violence.

A cyber incident between Israel and Iran similarly illustrates the attractiveness of cyber operations as a capability to engage in limited, hostile activities. In 2020, Israel accused Iran of conducting a cyber operation against Israeli water treatment facilities that, if the operation had succeeded, might have harmed people and damaged property. Israel responded with a cyberattack that disrupted the operations of an Iranian port facility. Based on what is publicly known, both cyber operations probably remained below the use-of-force threshold. However, both countries engaged in calibrated cyber hostilities that did not escalate into armed conflict.

Whether states continue to keep the consequences of cyber operations below the use-of-force threshold remains to be seen. Political calculations might change. Governments might be more willing to probe where state practice will draw the use-of-force and armed-attack lines for higher-consequence cyber operations. The *Tallinn Manual 2.0* observed that '[t]he case of cyber operations that do not result in injury, death, damage, or destruction, but that otherwise have extensive negative effects, remains unsettled' (342). As noted above, state reactions to Stuxnet did not align with doctrinal application of the prohibition on the use of force, leaving open the possibility that states might interpret certain kinds of cyber-inflicted damage as falling below the use-of-force and armed-attack thresholds. Conversely, hostile cyber operations below the use-of-force threshold might continue to proliferate, producing incentives for states to adopt specific rules for this type of cyber conflict.

6.3.4 Anticipatory self-defence

Under international law, an imminent armed attack also triggers a state's right to use force in self-defence. This right of anticipatory self-defence has been controversial because states have disagreed about what 'imminent' means. The narrow interpretation is that an armed attack is imminent only if it is about to be launched. The broad perspective is that a state can use force to prevent a state or terrorist group from planning armed attacks or acquiring dangerous weapons, such as weapons of mass destruction. In between these positions is the 'last feasible window of opportunity' concept under which a state may exercise the right of anticipatory self-defence 'when the attacker is clearly committed to launching an armed attack and the victim State will lose its opportunity to effectively defend itself unless it acts' (*Tallinn Manual 2.0*, 351).

A state could exercise the right of anticipatory self-defence by using proportionate force through cyber operations against an imminent kinetic or cyber armed attack. A state could also use proportionate kinetic force against an imminent cyber armed attack. However, whether a state could identify that a foreign cyber operation constituted an imminent armed attack is doubtful. The growth of cybercrime and cyber espionage demonstrates that countries have difficulty identifying when hostile cyber operations are in progress. How governments would be better at spotting cyber operations that might constitute an imminent armed attack is not clear. In addition, determining in advance that a foreign cyber operation would, if launched, create effects on a scale to qualify as an armed attack would be difficult given the range of consequences cyber operations can create. If a state identified hostile cyber activities under preparation in another country, it could attempt to disrupt those activities through cyber operations beneath the use-of-force threshold and not have to rely on the right to use force in anticipatory self-defence.

The cyber incident often discussed under the right of anticipatory self-defence is Stuxnet. Israel and the United States launched a cyber operation that, arguably, constituted a use of force to degrade Iran's ability to develop nuclear weapons. Justifying this operation under the right of anticipatory self-defence requires interpreting this right to permit using force to prevent countries from developing such weapons. Such a broad reading of the right remains controversial. If such an expansive right exists, Stuxnet could be seen as a proportionate use of force given the precise, limited, and non-lethal damage it caused. Stuxnet demonstrated the utility of cyber weapons in exercising the right of anticipatory self-defence, providing another reason why states find offensive cyber capabilities attractive. If Stuxnet was not a use of force, then Israel and the United States did not need the right of anticipatory self-defence to justify the operation. The ambiguity in state reactions to Stuxnet might have involved governments hedging their bets because cyber operations have potential above and below the use-of-force threshold.

The US cyberattack in 2019 against Iran that reportedly wiped out a database ostensibly used to plan Iranian attacks on oil tankers in the Persian Gulf (see above) provides material for applying the right of anticipatory self-defence to cyber operations. This incident raises the question whether a cyber operation that apparently damaged or destroyed a database crossed the use-of-force threshold. If it did not, then the United States would not need the right of anticipatory self-defence to justify it under international law. If the cyberattack qualified as a use of force, then the United States could appeal to the right of anticipatory self-defence if an attack on a US flagged vessel in the Persian Gulf was imminent. Based on what is known, the cyber operation sought to prevent future attacks on ships flagged to various nations, which raises collective self-defence issues, rather than to stop imminent attacks on US vessels, which touches on the controversy about the scope of imminence under the right of anticipatory self-defence.[10]

6.3.5 The principles on state responsibility

In responding to an illegal use of force with countermeasures, or in using force in self-defence against an actual or imminent armed attack, a state must establish that the country targeted is responsible for the use of force or armed attack.[11] Under international law, '[c]yber operations conducted by organs of a State, or by persons or entities empowered by domestic law to exercise elements of governmental authority, are attributable to the State' (*Tallinn Manual 2.0*, Rule 15). Attributing a cyber operation to a state can be difficult because cyber technologies permit states to disguise their involvement. States sometimes outsource cyber operations to non-state actors, which also exploit technical tricks to hide the origin of the operations. A state is responsible for cyber operations conducted by non-state actors when the state (1) instructs, directs, or controls the oper-

---

[10] Other cyber incidents with anticipatory features did not involve imminent attacks or uses of force. During its 2018 elections, the United States conducted cyber operations not amounting to a use of force to disrupt Russian disinformation campaigns that did not constitute an imminent armed attack or a use of force.

[11] See also the discussion of the international law on state responsibility in connection with terrorism in Section 4.5.2; and Constantine Antonopoulos, 'State Responsibility in Cyberspace', in *Research Handbook on International Law and Cyberspace*, 113–29.

ations; or (2) acknowledges the operations as its own (*Tallinn Manual 2.0*, Rule 17).

6.3.6 The act and crime of aggression

States have defined and criminalized 'aggression' under international law.[12] The Rome Statute of the International Criminal Court (1998) gave the International Criminal Court (ICC) jurisdiction over the crime of aggression (art. 5(2)), but the statute did not initially define this crime. In 2010, ICC states parties amended the treaty to include definitions for an 'act of aggression' and the 'crime of aggression'.

An act of aggression 'means the use of armed force by a State against the sovereignty, territorial integrity or political independence of another State, or in any other manner inconsistent with the Charter of the United Nations' (Rome Statute, art. 8*bis*, sec. 2). This language resembles the prohibition of the use of force (Section 6.3.2), indicating that an illegal use of force constitutes an act of aggression. Under the amendment, 'the use of any weapons by a State against the territory of another State' qualifies as an act of aggression (Rome Statute, 8*bis*, sec. 2(b)), which would encompass use of cyber weapons.

A crime of aggression 'means the planning, preparation, initiation or execution ... of an act of aggression which, by its character, gravity and scale, constitutes a manifest violation of the Charter of the United Nations' (Rome Statute, art. 8*bis*, sec. 1). The emphasis on the gravity and scale of an act of aggression tracks the severity required for a use of force to be an armed attack (Section 6.3.2). Absent a legal justification, armed attacks that trigger a state's right to use force in self-defence are manifest violations of the UN Charter. Thus, not every act of aggression is a crime. Persons who have effective control over, or direction of, the actions of a state that constitute a crime of aggression are criminally accountable (Rome Statute, art. 8*bis*, sec. 1).

At least for states parties that accept these amendments, the ICC could prosecute persons responsible for controlling or directing cyber opera-

---

[12] For criminal responsibility under international humanitarian law, see Kai Ambos, 'International Criminal Responsibility in Cyberspace', in *Research Handbook on International Law and Cyberspace*, 152–80.

tions the gravity and scale of which manifestly violate the UN Charter. To date, no known cyber operations have been serious enough to constitute a crime of aggression. Leaving aside that Iran, Israel, and the United States are not ICC states parties, the Stuxnet operation would, at most, qualify as an act of aggression as, arguably, an illegal use of force. Nevertheless, cyber operations that could constitute a crime of aggression can be imagined.

The ICC can exercise jurisdiction over conduct that occurs on the territory of a state party (Rome Statute, art. 12(2)(a)). Nothing in the Rome Statute suggests that cyber operations are excluded from this territorial jurisdiction. The ICC has ruled that its jurisdiction covers conduct in a state party's territory by the armed forces of states not party to the Rome Statute (ICC-02/17-138 (2020)). Applying the ICC's jurisdiction to the actions of military forces of states that have not joined the ICC is controversial, but the court's willingness to exercise its authority in this way has relevance for cyber operations. The ICC could exercise jurisdiction over a cyber operation by a state not party to the Rome Statute launched from, or that takes effective control over targets in, an ICC state party if that operation is potentially a crime under the Rome Statute, including the crime of aggression.

6.3.7   Security Council authorization of the use of force

The Security Council can authorize UN members to use force to counter a threat to international peace and security (UN Charter, arts 39 and 42). The Security Council process is political not legal in nature, which means that the five permanent, veto-wielding members determine whether the council exercises this authority. However, if the Security Council authorizes UN members to use force, then the members do not need any other justification under international law.

A Security Council authorization to use of force empowers UN members to take all necessary means or measures, including cyber operations (*Tallinn Manual 2.0*, Rule 76), if the operations support the objectives established by the Security Council and comply with international humanitarian law. In 2011, the Security Council authorized UN members to take all necessary measures to protect civilians under threat of attack in Libya. The US government considered, but ultimately rejected, cyber-attacks on Libyan air defences. Given the kinetic force used under the Security Council's authorization, such cyberattacks conducted to protect civilians and compliant with international humanitarian law would have been lawful.

6.3.8 Humanitarian intervention

Whether states can use force to stop or prevent large-scale atrocities without Security Council authorization has been contentious for decades. During the Cold War, military operations justified as humanitarian interventions – but not authorized by the Security Council – generated controversy because they often had geopolitical or ideological motives rather than humanitarian ones. After the Cold War, the Security Council authorized the use of force in response to some humanitarian crises, but disagreement persisted on whether states could use force for humanitarian intervention absent Security Council permission.

In 1999, NATO members argued that international law allowed them to use of force to stop atrocities in Kosovo without Security Council authorization and without the right to use force in self-defence being applicable. This crisis sparked the development of the responsibility to protect (R2P) principle, a purported emerging norm that permits states to use force in another country if its government fails to protect its population from large-scale violence or harms. In 2005, most UN members agreed that the Security Council must authorize the use of force under the R2P principle, continuing the controversy about the use of force and humanitarian intervention.

A Security Council authorization to use force would authorize UN members to use kinetic and cyber capabilities in a humanitarian intervention. In addition, states could act against imminent or actual atrocities without the need for the Security Council to authorize the use of force by conducting cyber operations that fall below the use-of-force threshold. However, cyber operations alone are unlikely to prevent or stop the atrocities that trigger the R2P principle. The need for kinetic force in these situations means the controversy about the use of force for humanitarian intervention without Security Council authorization will continue.

6.3.9 Cyber operations not constituting uses of force

As noted above, cyber operations other than Stuxnet have not generated serious and sustained debates about whether they qualified as uses of force or armed attacks. The number and variety of cyber operations that go beyond or do not involve espionage – ranging from disinformation campaigns to covert cyber actions – suggest that states are engaging in cyber coercion under the use-of-force threshold.[13] This realm of cyber hostilities raises questions about other rules, such as sovereignty and non-intervention, as well as the adequacy of the responses that international law permits to cyber violations of these rules.[14]

International law on sovereignty and non-intervention often proved difficult to apply in the pre-cyber world. The emergence of cyber operations by states has allowed the older controversies to resurface in the context of new technologies that permit diverse operations and consequences. States acknowledge that international law on sovereignty and non-intervention applies to the cyber operations of states. How these rules apply in the cyber context highlights again the importance of setting and applying legal thresholds – when does a cyber operation violate a country's sovereignty, and when does a violation of sovereignty become an illegal intervention? (See Figure 6.1) States have largely been unwilling to make clear how the international law on sovereignty and non-intervention applies in cyberspace. The lack of state practice has hampered efforts to determine when cyber operations violate these rules of international law.

Sovereignty

Generally, states agree that '[t]he principle of State sovereignty applies in cyberspace' and '[a] State must not conduct cyber operations that violate the sovereignty of another State' (*Tallinn Manual 2.0*, Rules 1 and 4). However, in 2018, the UK government argued that sovereignty was only a general principle and not a rule that prohibits cyber activities in a state without its consent. This position leaves the international law on non-intervention to govern cyber operations not amounting to a use of force. A debate ensued about whether sovereignty is a general principle or a rule in international law. The legal arguments and state practice

---

13   The range of cyber operations that states can conduct under the use-of-force threshold includes operations that are not cybersecurity threats as defined in this book, such as information and disinformation operations.

14   See also discussion of the international law on sovereignty and non-intervention concerning internet governance (Section 2.2), cybersecurity governance (Section 2.4), cybercrime (Section 3.3.1), cyber espionage (Section 5.2), and covert cyber action (Section 5.4).

favoured interpreting sovereignty as a rule, but this conclusion does not clarify when cyber operations violate sovereignty.

To date, state practice does not reveal agreement on where to set the sovereignty threshold or what criteria to use in evaluating the consequences of a cyber operation. In its statement on *International Law Applied to Operations in Cyberspace* (2019), France set the threshold low by claiming that any 'cyberattack against French digital systems or any effects produced on French territory by digital means by a State … constitutes a breach of sovereignty' (sec. 1.1.1). This position echoes the internet and cyber-sovereignty concepts used by China, Russia, and other authoritarian states. Other countries do not take this strict approach to sovereignty. The *Basic Position of the Government of Japan on International Law Applicable to Cyber Operations* (2021) stated that cyber operations 'causing physical damage or loss of functionality … against critical infrastructure … may constitute a violation of sovereignty' (3). In addition, many states simply have not taken a public position on when cyber operations violate sovereignty.

Based on what can be gleaned from state practice, determining whether a cyber operation violates a state's sovereignty involves a case-by-case evaluation of the type of operation, its scale, and the severity of the effects it causes, including physical damage, loss of functionality, or interference with inherently governmental functions.[15] This evaluation assumes that a cyber operation does not violate sovereignty unless it crosses some threshold of quantitative and qualitative effects. Stuxnet violated Iranian sovereignty given the extensive physical damage it caused; but, as noted above, the Stuxnet operation remains an outlier among cyber operations conducted by states. Beyond the need for a case-by-case evaluation, state practice exhibits no consensus on how to determine whether a cyber operation violates sovereignty.

---

[15]   See also how international law applies to cyber espionage (Section 5.2), namely that it does not *per se* violate international law, including the rules on sovereignty and non-intervention, but that the methods by which a state conducts cyber espionage might do so.

Non-intervention

As with sovereignty, states agree that the prohibition on intervention into the domestic affairs of other states applies in cyberspace (*Tallinn Manual 2.0*, Rule 66). Although this rule proved difficult to apply in the pre-cyber era, the criteria for determining on a case-by-case basis whether a state violated it are established. To constitute an illegal intervention, a state's act must be coercive concerning matters over which another state has sovereign authority, such as its political system and foreign policy. Coercive acts interfere with a state's free exercise of its sovereignty by forcing, or attempting to force, a change in that state's behaviour or its ability to control matters over which it has sovereign authority. However, to date, state practice provides little clarity on how the non-intervention rule applies to cyber operations. Few cyber incidents have approached the threshold of a coercive act that interferes with a state's exercise of sovereignty, and governments have been reluctant to apply the rule to cyber incidents that might have crossed that threshold.

Stuxnet involved a coercive act that interfered with Iran's ability to control activities over which it had sovereign authority. As an exceptional incident, Stuxnet does not illuminate when different and less consequential cyber operations cross the intervention threshold. Cyber espionage 'does not qualify as intervention because it lacks a coercive element' (*Tallinn Manual 2.0*, 323). Government pronouncements about how international law applies in cyberspace tend to be general on non-intervention. New Zealand's statement on *The Application of International Law to State Activity in Cyberspace* (2020) restates the non-intervention rule and lists examples of cyber activities that might violate the rule (paras 9 and 10).

For many experts, few cyber operations conducted by states approach the intervention threshold because most only implicate state sovereignty (see above). Cyber incidents that arguably crossed the intervention threshold either did not produce specific accusations of intervention from victim states or generated disagreements about whether the non-intervention rule had been violated. Certainly, cyber operations that would constitute illegal intervention can be conceived, such as cyber interference that changes election outcomes. But such clear-cut incidents do not characterize the cyber operations that states have undertaken to date.

Responding to violations of the sovereignty and non-intervention rules

States that experience cyber operations that violate the rules on sovereignty or non-intervention can implement peaceful, proportionate countermeasures against the state that conducted the operations, as identified under the international law on state responsibility. Countermeasures could involve, but are not limited to, proportionate cyber operations designed to bring the state responsible for violating international law back into compliance with its obligations. For example, the United States purportedly conducted proportionate cyber operations against North Korea in response to North Korean cyber activities against Sony Entertainment in 2014. The Israeli cyber operation in 2020 against an Iranian port facility could be interpreted as a proportionate response to Iran's cyber operation against Israeli water treatment facilities. The US and Israeli cyber operations can be viewed as countermeasures under international law, if the North Korean and Iranian actions violated US and Israeli sovereignty.

The frequency of cyber operations conducted beneath the use-of-force threshold has raised concerns that the right to implement countermeasures in response to internationally wrongful acts is an insufficient remedy. The law on countermeasures does not apply to cyber espionage – the most ubiquitous cyber activity conducted by states under the use-of-force threshold – because cyber espionage does not, *per se*, violate the rules on sovereignty and non-intervention (Section 5.2.1). Online propaganda and disinformation also do not violate these principles, which takes countermeasures off the table and leaves retorsion – unfriendly but lawful acts – as the remedy.[16] The reluctance of states to clarify when cyber operations violate sovereignty and the prohibition on intervention creates confusion whether victim-state responses to such operations represent countermeasures or retorsion.

This muddled legal patchwork increases the incentives that states possess to conduct cyber operations below the use-of-force level, which increases cybersecurity threats for the public and private sectors. Countermeasures

---

[16] For example, the United States did not claim that Russia violated international law in conducting its hack-and-leak campaign during the US elections in 2016. Neither the hack (cyber espionage) nor the leak (information operations) violated the rules on sovereignty and non-intervention. Measures taken by the United States against Russia after this incident, such as sanctions, constituted retorsion rather than countermeasures.

and retorsion have not stemmed the flood of hostile cyber operations that are not uses of force. Instead, the argument goes, states should pursue deterrence by punishment – retaliate and inflict disproportionate costs on governments that launch cyber operations beneath the use-of-force threshold. This approach does not require determining whether a cyber operation violates international law and focuses on deterring harmful cyber operations by threatening to punish perpetrators. As a strategy, deterrence by punishment is controversial for several reasons, including the risks of escalating cyber hostilities and marginalizing international law's role in cybersecurity. Nevertheless, the perceived failure of deterrence by norms (international law) and deterrence by denial (cyber defence) to contain cyber hostilities below the use of force keeps political interest in deterrence by punishment a robust and persistent feature of cybersecurity debates.[17]

6.4   Fighting armed conflict in cyberspace

The second category of issues to analyse in the relationship between cyber operations and war involves the international law that governs how states engage in armed conflict. These rules go by different monikers – the laws of war, *jus in bello*, law of armed conflict, and international humanitarian law (IHL). This area of international law has a long history and contains many rules that emerged through customary international law and treaties.[18] This section focuses on the most important rules applicable to cyber operations in armed conflict, but, unlike the *Tallinn Manual 2.0*, it is not a comprehensive treatment of IHL's application to cyber operations.

6.4.1   Background on international humanitarian law

IHL applies when an 'armed conflict' exists, which happens when a state or non-state actor engages in sustained military or other hostilities that cause injury or death to people and damage or destruction to property.

---

[17]   See also the interest in using offensive cyber operations against cybercriminal groups and states that provide havens for such groups discussed in Section 3.4.4.

[18]   The ICRC provides excellent resources on IHL, including databases on treaties, customary international law, and national implementation.

Isolated, limited incidents – such as brief border clashes, one-off covert actions, small-scale terrorist attacks, and criminal violence – are not armed conflicts. The level and duration of violence required for hostilities to cross the armed-conflict threshold has been the subject of disagreement. Even so, the case-by-case determination of when hostilities become armed conflict has not been as problematical as deciding when state actions have crossed the thresholds on the use of force, armed attack, sovereignty, and intervention (Section 6.3). Whether an armed conflict exists has been most controversial in non-international hostilities, such as civil wars, when governments often oppose applying IHL to insurgents (Section 6.4.4).[19]

At the core of IHL is the norm that the right to choose how to injure the enemy is not unlimited. This idea informs principles that regulate international and non-international armed conflict. IHL recognizes a belligerent's right to use force (principle of military necessity) that is proportionate as between the military advantages sought and the incidental civilian damage done (principle of proportionality) and that can be and is directed at legitimate military targets (principles of distinction and discrimination).[20] Belligerents cannot use force in ways that create superfluous injury or unnecessary suffering (principle of humanity), are dishonourable (principle of chivalry), or – in international armed conflict – that violate the rights of states not involved in the conflict (principle of neutrality). These principles apply when a belligerent engages in an 'attack' – offensive or defensive violence against the adversary intended to, or that would foreseeably, cause injury and death to people or damage and destruction to property (Figure 6.2).

Historically, states have applied these principles to attacks no matter what technologies militaries used. Whether states could use nuclear weapons in compliance with IHL has been contentious, but the controversy has not involved arguments that the use of nuclear weapons in armed conflict escapes IHL. States have banned certain technologies from armed conflict

---

[19]   On distinguishing international from non-international armed conflict, see Louise Arimatsu, 'Classifying Cyber Warfare', in *Research Handbook on International Law and Cyberspace*, 405–25.

[20]   See Terry D. Gill, 'International Humanitarian Law Applied to Cyber-Warfare: Precautions, Proportionality and the Notion of "Attack" under the Humanitarian Law of Armed Conflict', in *Research Handbook on International Law and Cyberspace*, 456–69.

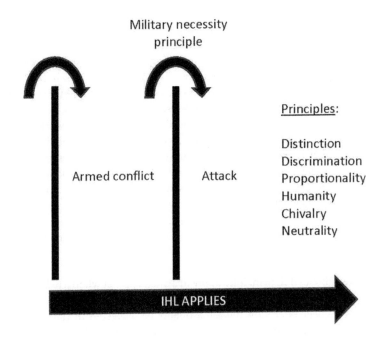

Figure 6.2   The armed conflict and attack thresholds in international humanitarian law

(Section 6.5.1), but IHL applies to all means and methods of warfare used to engage in attacks.

6.4.2   Cyber operations and armed conflict

Cyber operations conducted without other hostile activities could create an armed conflict if the operations produce sufficient injury, death, damage, or destruction. So far, cyber operations have not triggered an armed conflict. Stuxnet is the only incident that has tested the armed-conflict threshold. The International Group of Experts that produced the Tallinn manuals could not agree on whether Stuxnet caused enough damage to create an armed conflict (*Tallinn Manual 2.0*, 384). States did not act as if Stuxnet created an armed conflict between the countries involved. The state practice suggests that Stuxnet fell below the armed-conflict threshold, like acts of covert sabotage have done in the past. Cyber operations that would stand alone as acts of war, such as a 'cyber Pearl Harbor' attack, can be imagined but, as noted above, the most likely scenario is that kinetic hostilities will be involved in initiating armed conflict.

When an armed conflict exists, most states agree that IHL applies to cyber operations conducted during that armed conflict (*Tallinn Manual 2.0*, Rule 80). This view conforms with the historical application of IHL to all means and methods of waging war. Even so, whether IHL applies to cyber operations in armed conflict has produced controversy. In the work of the UN Group of Governmental Experts (UNGGE), China prevented reports in 2013 and 2017 from including IHL in statements about the application of international law in cyberspace, ostensibly because China did not want to legitimize armed conflict in cyberspace.[21] However, IHL applies to armed conflicts whether they begin legally (e.g., under a Security Council authorization) or illegally (e.g., through an act of aggression). IHL's application to an armed conflict does not legitimize the conflict in any domain of hostilities.

As noted above, IHL principles apply in armed conflict when a belligerent engages in an attack. To qualify as an attack under IHL, an offensive or defensive cyber operation must reasonably be 'expected to cause injury or death to persons or damage or destruction to objects' (*Tallinn Manual 2.0*, Rule 92). Whether a hostile act in armed conflict is an attack is determined through a case-by-case analysis of the act's context, character, and consequences. As seen with the thresholds on the use of force and armed attack (Section 6.3.2), the diversity of cyber operations and their potential consequences mean many cyber operations during armed conflict will not be attacks, including cyber espionage, information operations, and low-consequence actions. In addition, determining when cyber operations cross the attack threshold will be challenging and potentially controversial.

Stuxnet proves useful in probing these observations. If we assume that an armed conflict existed, the Stuxnet operation would have constituted an attack under IHL given the hundreds of centrifuges it intended to, and

---

[21] The UNGGE's report in 2015 referenced the principles of necessity, proportionality, distinction, and humanity, but the report was not clear whether consensus was reached on the existence of these principles or the applicability of these principles in cyberspace.

did, damage. The operation would have been subject to the IHL principles that apply to attacks. However, cyber operations can produce consequences below the physical damage caused by Stuxnet, such as interfering with the functionality of computers. Analysing cyber operations requires assessing their intended, foreseeable, direct, and indirect effects, but this requirement does not make determining when a cyber operation qualifies as an attack easier. In the Tallinn process, for example, the International Group of Experts did not reach consensus on whether cyber interference with the functionality of objects constituted an attack under IHL (*Tallinn Manual 2.0*, 417–18). The lack of state practice on cyber operations in armed conflict continues to make the threshold-drawing exercise speculative.

The challenges of applying the attack threshold to cyber operations create concerns in connection with civilian use of cyberspace. The principle of distinction prohibits belligerents from intentionally attacking civilians and civilian objects.[22] This principle would not apply to cyber operations deemed to fall short of being attacks. Where the attack threshold is drawn will determine how much a belligerent could conduct cyber operations against civilian targets without the IHL rules on attacks applying. The dependence of civilians on cyberspace creates a target-rich environment during armed conflict for cyber operations that do not qualify as attacks. The International Committee of the Red Cross (ICRC) is particularly worried about the vulnerability of civilian populations to cyber operations during armed conflict.[23]

If a cyber operation constitutes an attack, then the operation is subject to IHL. Under the principle of military necessity, a belligerent can only use the amount of force required for the submission or defeat of the enemy. Given that this principle permits the use of kinetic force, a belligerent's use of cyber operations probably will not create controversy. However, if a belligerent can achieve military objectives with less injury, death,

---

22   On the principle of distinction, see Karine Bannelier, 'Is the Principle of Distinction Still Relevant in Cyberwarfare? From Doctrinal Discourse to States' Practice', in *Research Handbook on International Law and Cyberspace*, 426–55.

23   See Laurent Gisel, Tilman Rodenhäuser, and Knut Dörmann, 'Twenty Years On: International Humanitarian Law and the Protection of Civilians against the Effects of Cyber Operations during Armed Conflicts', *International Review of the Red Cross* 103(913) (2020): 287–334.

damage, and destruction through cyber operations, does this capability mean the principle of military necessity would require the use of cyber means over kinetic munitions? States have resisted reading into IHL any general requirement to use less lethal and destructive weapons in armed conflict, so state practice is unlikely to develop in ways that impose such an obligation. The integration of cyber capabilities into military forces also means that attacks in armed conflict will increasingly involve coordinated kinetic and cyber operations.

A cyberattack must also comply with the IHL principles summarized in Table 6.1, which includes the corresponding rules from the *Tallinn Manual 2.0*. The different nature of cyber capabilities most directly affects the principles of humanity and neutrality. Cyber operations would rarely, if ever, produce superfluous injury or unnecessary suffering for persons, which means the principle of humanity is unlikely to present problems.

By contrast, the technologies that create cyberspace produce challenges for the principle of neutrality in international armed conflict.[24] Would a belligerent violate this principle if all or part of a cyberattack, such as Stuxnet, was transmitted through the cyber infrastructure of neutral states? For many, the internet makes it difficult, if not impossible, for a belligerent to prevent all data packets in a cyber weapon from being transmitted through cyber infrastructure in neutral states. For the US Department of Defense, routing a cyber weapon through a neutral state's cyber infrastructure without causing damage would not violate the neutrality principle. The practice of states that have launched cyber operations during armed conflicts (Sections 6.4.3 and 6.4.4) probably supports this view. However, in the Tallinn process, most of the International Group of Experts believed that transmitting a cyber weapon across a neutral state's cyber infrastructure violated the neutrality principle (*Tallinn Manual 2.0*, 557).

Stuxnet illuminates how belligerents can execute cyberattacks that comply with IHL. Assuming there was an armed conflict, the Stuxnet operation attacked a military target – facilities associated with the development of nuclear weapons. The cyber weapon was not indiscriminate because it only damaged specific machinery. The attack produced no collateral

---

[24] See David Turns, 'Cyber War and the Law of Neutrality', in *Research Handbook on International Law and Cyberspace*, 470–88.

Table 6.1   Principles of international humanitarian law applicable
to cyberattacks in armed conflict

Basic Description of the Principle	Summary of the Applicable Rule in the *Tallinn Manual 2.0*
Principle of distinction	
Belligerent attacks must distinguish between legitimate and protected targets.	*Rule 94 – Prohibition on attacking civilians*: The civilian population, as well as individual civilians, shall not be the object of cyberattack.
Principle of discrimination	
Belligerent means and methods of attack must be able to discriminate between legitimate military objectives and non-combatants.	*Rule 105 – Indiscriminate means or methods*: Means or methods of cyber warfare that are indiscriminate are prohibited. Such means and methods are indiscriminate when they cannot be: (a) directed at a specific military objective; or (b) limited in their effects as required by IHL. Such indiscriminate means and methods are likely to strike military objectives and civilians or civilian objects without distinction.
Principle of proportionality	
Belligerent force must be proportionate to the military threat faced and the military value of the target of the attack.	*Rule 113 – Proportionality*: A cyberattack that may be expected to cause incidental loss of civilian life, injury to civilians, damage to civilian objects, or a combination thereof, that would be excessive in relation to the military advantage anticipated is prohibited.
Principle of humanity	
Belligerent means and methods cannot cause superfluous injury of unnecessary suffering (e.g., expanding bullets, blinding lasers, and weapons that injure through non-detectable fragments).	*Rule 104 – Superfluous injury or unnecessary suffering*: Means and methods of cyber warfare that cause superfluous injury or unnecessary suffering are prohibited.

Principle of chivalry	
Belligerents cannot employ treacherous or perfidious means and methods in armed conflict.	*Rule 122 – Perfidy*: Cyber operations that kill or injure an adversary through perfidy are prohibited. Acts that invite an adversary's confidence – undertaken with the intent to betray such confidence – and that lead the adversary to believe he or she is entitled to receive, or must provide, protection under IHL constitute perfidy.
Principle of neutrality (international armed conflict only)	
States not engaged in armed conflict have a right to be left alone by the belligerents, if those states preserve their neutrality.	*Rule 151 – Cyber operations in neutral territory*: Exercising belligerent rights in neutral territory by cyber means is prohibited.

damage for civilians or civilian objects inside or outside Iran and was proportionate to the military value of the target. The malware spread beyond the target, but it did not damage computers, networks, or machinery inside or outside Iran. The aspects of the operation that involved disguising the attack were permitted ruses of war not perfidious acts.

Cyber operations can also violate IHL. Belligerents could launch cyberattacks intentionally against civilian targets and breach the principle of distinction. Poorly designed malware can disseminate beyond the target and cause damage that violates the principle of discrimination. Discriminate cyber operations against military targets might cause excessive collateral damage to civilian objects, violating the principle of proportionality. Cyber technologies provide opportunities for perfidy. A belligerent could invite an adversary's confidence by sending fake electronic mail purporting to be from the ICRC concerning an issue protected under IHL, such as treating wounded combatants, with the intent to betray that confidence by injuring or killing the adversary in an ambush.

Efforts to identify how IHL applies to cyber operations have involved concerns about the protection of civilians and civilian objects. These concerns reflect how cyber technologies potentially increase the likelihood of attacks against, or adverse consequences for, civilians. IHL permits attacks on civilians who directly participate in hostilities and on objects that serve military and civilian purposes, so-called 'dual-use objects'. The interconnectedness of cyber technologies, such as military use of civilian-operated cyber infrastructure, creates questions about what constitutes direct civilian participation in hostilities and what qualifies as a dual-use object. In addition, whether IHL protects civilian data in the same way it protects civilian objects has generated debate.

The challenges that cyber technologies present for the protection of civilians and civilian objects are real but should be kept in perspective. Attacks on civilians directly participating in hostilities and on dual-use objects must comply with IHL, including the principles of discrimination and proportionality. Belligerents launching attacks must also take all feasible precautions to avoid and minimize incidental injury to civilians, loss of civilian life, and damage to civilian objects (*Tallinn Manual 2.0*, Rule 116). States must conduct legal reviews of cyber means of armed conflict to ensure they comply with IHL (*Tallinn Manual 2.0*, Rule 110(a)).[25] In addition, the principle of proportionality permits a belligerent to cause foreseeable injury, death, damage, or destruction to civilians or civilian objects if those consequences are proportionate to the military advantage anticipated from attacking a legitimate target (*Tallinn Manual 2.0*, Rule 113). A cyber operation might damage a dual-use object, disrupt the activities of civilians participating in hostilities, and produce collateral damage with less harmful civilian consequences than lawful kinetic attacks. This potentiality further underscores why cyber weapons and operations are attractive means and methods of warfare under IHL.

Certain acts that violate IHL constitute crimes under international law. The need to support IHL with criminal sanctions has long been recognized, as illustrated by the war crimes tribunals created after World War II. The Security Council's establishment of war crimes tribunals in the 1990s to prosecute IHL violations in the former Yugoslavia and Rwanda advanced the cause of international criminal law. The ICC's establishment in 1998 constituted a landmark. The ICC has jurisdiction over the crime of genocide, crimes against humanity, war crimes, and the crime of aggression (Rome Statute, art. 5) (Section 6.3.6).

Given the Rome Statute's definitions, committing the crime of genocide and crimes against humanity through cyber technologies would be diffi-

---

[25] For states parties to Additional Protocol I (1977) to the Geneva Conventions of 1949, the obligation to conduct a legal review applies to cyber methods as well as cyber means of warfare (*Tallinn Manual 2.0*, Rule 110(b)).

cult, if not impossible, because perpetrators of these crimes must engage in killing, injuring, enslaving, or torturing people on a significant scale. Cyber operations could support genocide and crimes against humanity by being used to disseminate propaganda to advance plans to commit atrocities. Cyber operations could constitute war crimes because a belligerent might, for example, intentionally use a cyber weapon to damage civilian objects, such as hospitals, and knowingly cause civilian injury and death (Rome Statute, art. 8(2)(b)(ii) and (ix)). In addition, cyber operations could be perfidious, which is a war crime (Rome Statute, art. 8(2)(b)(vii)). Military commanders and political superiors who order cyber operations that constitute war crimes are responsible for such crimes; and military commanders who knew, or should have known, that subordinates were preparing to commit, were committing, or had committed war crimes and failed to take reasonable and feasible preventive or punitive measures are criminally responsible (*Tallinn Manual 2.0*, Rule 85).

6.4.3   Cyber operations during international armed conflict

Cyber operations have occurred in international armed conflicts. Before the US invasion of Iraq in 2003, the United States infiltrated Iraq's military computers to engage in information operations against Iraqi military personnel. Such operations were not an attack under IHL. In 2007, Israel executed a cyber-facilitated ruse to trick Syrian air defence systems as part of an Israeli air assault on a suspected Syrian nuclear weapons facility. The IHL issues in this incident did not arise from the cyber operations, which did not constitute an attack or perfidy.

In 2008, DDoS and website-defacement operations occurred during the armed conflict between Georgia and Russia. Whether these operations were attributable to Russia under the international law on state responsibility remained contentious. It was also unlikely that the DDoS and website-defacement operations qualified as attacks under IHL, even though some of these operations targeted civilian computers, networks, and websites. In response, Georgia used companies in the United States to operate government websites, which raised questions about whether it violated the principle of neutrality by setting up communication facilities in a neutral country.

Cyber operations have also happened during the armed conflict between Russia and the Ukraine in eastern Ukraine. Many of these operations have fallen below IHL's attack threshold because they involved espionage, information operations, or temporary disruption of cyber services. However, a cyber operation in 2015 against Ukrainian electrical power infrastructure disrupted electricity supplies to thousands of people during winter. Yet, attributing responsibility for the operation to Russia faced difficulties, as did determining whether the disruption of electricity supplies qualified as an attack under IHL.

These examples demonstrate that, so far, cyber operations during international armed conflict have not caused the kind of IHL problems associated with kinetic military activities. However, as military forces enhance their cyber capabilities and civilian dependence on cyberspace deepens, cyber operations might begin to stress IHL during international armed conflict and force a reckoning among states concerning attribution, the attack threshold, dual-use objects, and targeting civilian objects and data.

6.4.4   Cyber operations during non-international armed conflict

Since World War II, non-international armed conflicts, such as civil wars, have challenged IHL. A 'non-international armed conflict exists whenever there is protracted armed violence … between governmental armed forces and organised armed groups, or between such groups' that reaches 'a minimum level of intensity and the parties involved in the conflict … have a minimum degree of organisation' (*Tallinn Manual 2.0*, Rule 83). Non-international armed conflicts are unlikely to be triggered by, or conducted primarily through, cyber operations. Except for the principle of neutrality, the IHL rules on attacks in Table 6.1 apply in non-international armed conflicts and encounter the same issues. However, governments often resist applying IHL in non-international armed conflicts to avoid giving insurgents the status and rights that IHL provides them.

The non-international armed conflict fought between the Islamic State terrorist group and the military forces of a coalition of countries beginning in 2014 involved cyber operations acknowledged by Australia, the United States, and the UK. However, these countries did not provide sufficient information about the operations or their consequences to permit a thorough IHL analysis. Based on what was disclosed, the cyber operations either (1) disrupted or damaged the Islamic State's military command, control, and communication capabilities in supporting kinetic attacks against the Islamic State; or (2) disrupted the Islamic State's online activities, such as the dissemination of propaganda, in ways that did not constitute attacks under IHL.

As far as is known, the cyber operations against the Islamic State did not create concerns that the operations violated IHL. Reflections on the US military's cyber operations against the Islamic State focused on their effectiveness, with US officials expressing disappointment in what the cyber operations achieved. Indeed, kinetic attacks on the Islamic State's military capabilities, combined with the Islamic State's loss of control over territory, did more to degrade the Islamic State's cyber activities than the cyber operations of coalition military forces.

The Islamic State's online dissemination of videos recording executions, beheadings, and crucifixions did not constitute attacks under IHL. However, the videos provided evidence that the Islamic State breached other IHL principles and committed war crimes by violating the dignity of detained persons, spreading terror among civilians, and constituting acts of terrorism directed at persons protected by IHL, including detainees and civilians. The way IHL applied to the Islamic State's atrocity videos demonstrates that IHL has relevance for cyber operations in armed conflict that do not constitute attacks.

6.5   Arms control and cyber weapons

Since the latter half of the nineteenth century, states have used international law to control, restrict, or prohibit certain weapons of war. Banned weapons include exploding bullets, biological and chemical weapons, blinding laser weapons, anti-personnel mines, and cluster munitions. States have also tried to limit the type and numbers of some weapons, especially nuclear weapons, to minimize the likelihood of war. Countries have used confidence-building measures, such as establishing crisis communication channels, and export restrictions to prevent the development, proliferation, and use of specific weapon technologies. Whether states should apply these approaches to cyber means and methods of armed conflict has stimulated debate.

6.5.1   Arms control strategies

Cyberspace proves a difficult context for techniques used to control other weapon technologies. The means for creating cyber weapons – computers, software, and programming skills – are globally disseminated. Countries around the world are developing offensive and defensive cyber capabilities. Controls or prohibitions would need to focus on cyber means and methods perceived to be dangerous, such as indiscriminate malware that can cause widespread harm. However, the international law on sovereignty and non-intervention already applies to cyber operations that do not cross the use-of-force threshold (Section 6.3.9). IHL prohibits cyber operations in armed conflict that would violate the principles of discrimination and proportionality (Section 6.4.2).

Outlawing specific cyber weaponry, such as malware that targets machinery running civilian critical infrastructure, would prove difficult because the same or similar machinery often operates within lawful military targets. Attempts to regulate how states manage zero-day vulnerabilities as part of controlling cyber weapons would confront the strong interests that governments possess to use such vulnerabilities for legitimate national security purposes (Section 5.3.3). Numerical limits make no sense because cyber weapons are easily replicated. Verification would prove difficult given the nature of cyber technologies. Without verification mechanisms, monitoring and enforcement of cyber arms control agreements would be impossible.

Using arms control for cyber technologies would confront other challenges. Many treaties that ban weapons were adopted because enough states concluded that the weapons prohibited had little military utility, were ethically repugnant, or both. By contrast, cyber weapons have military and ethical utility in armed conflict.[26] States used arms control agreements to stabilize nuclear deterrence by limiting the number of offensive weapons and banning the deployment of defensive anti-ballistic missile systems. However, nuclear deterrence is not a productive analogy for cybersecurity. Cyber deterrence requires states to have robust, full-spectrum offensive and defensive capabilities – a context not condu-

---

[26]   On the ethics of cyber weapons, see Neil C. Rowe, 'Distinctive Ethical Challenges of Cyberweapons', in *Research Handbook on International Law and Cyberspace*, 387–404.

cive for concluding international agreements that impose limitations on such capabilities.

6.5.2   Confidence-building measures

Confidence-building measures (CBMs) used in the contexts of conventional and nuclear weapons are another possible path for stabilizing competition in military cyber power. CBMs range from unilateral declarations of 'no first use' to mechanisms that increase transparency, reduce distrust, and enhance stability – such as crisis communications systems, routine diplomatic meetings, information-sharing arrangements, and provision of assistance to address perceived or actual threats. In 2013, the United States and Russia agreed to cyber CBMs, including a cyber 'hot line' between the White House and the Kremlin. International efforts to improve cybersecurity have often promoted the development of CBMs.

In non-cyber contexts, CBMs have an uneven track record and have not been a panacea for state competition over military power and geopolitical influence. The cyber context exhibits the same problems. The US–Russian CBM agreement broke down before the Russian cyber interference in the US elections in 2016. Efforts to build confidence in the cyber realm between the United States and China, such as the non-binding agreement on economic cyber espionage (Section 5.2.3), have failed. No CBMs have been agreed between countries engaging in cyber hostilities, such as between the United States, on the one hand, and North Korea and Iran, on the other.

6.5.3   Export control strategies

During the Cold War, Western states used export controls to stop the Soviet Union from obtaining civilian technologies that had military applications. After the Cold War, export control regimes, such as the Wassenaar Arrangement on Export Controls for Conventional Arms and Dual-Use Goods and Technologies, worked to prevent 'rogue' states and terrorists from getting access to dual-use technologies related to weapons of mass destruction. The utility of this approach for the cyber realm is questionable. The intelligence agencies and military forces of many states, companies that provide cybersecurity services, and cybercriminals already have the technologies and skills for conducting cyber operations.

A human rights effort to use the Wassenaar Arrangement to keep repressive regimes from obtaining surveillance and intrusion penetration software illustrates the difficulties of using export controls in the cyber context. The effort provoked criticism from the private sector and cyber-security researchers, created implementation challenges for governments, and required re-negotiation within the Wassenaar Arrangement. This attempt to use export controls has not prevented repressive governments from obtaining surveillance software for use against citizens, political opponents, journalists, democracy advocates, and foreign government officials.

Two developments in 2021 further highlight the difficulties of using export controls against cyber technologies. First, news broke that governments around the world were using spyware developed by an Israeli company to infiltrate the smartphones and mobile devices of activists, journalists, and foreign government officials. Second, the United States fined former employees of its National Security Agency for violating US export control laws by helping the United Arab Emirates develop hacking tools that it used against political opponents, dissidents, and journalists. The global hacker-for-hire problem underscores that export control laws have not prevented, and are unlikely to stem, the proliferation of software that governments use for repressive purposes at home and in offensive operations abroad.

7 Conclusion: Cybersecurity law in a divided world

7.1   Taking stock of cybersecurity law

The end of a decade encourages reflections on the recent past, and 2020 provided the opportunity to take stock of cybersecurity law after two, full decades of endeavours in this realm. History will remember 2020 primarily for the COVID-19 pandemic, but events during the year also captured so many issues in cybersecurity that it served as a microcosm for the field as a new decade began.

7.1.1   Cybersecurity and non-state actors: Cybercrime and cyber terrorism

In 2020, cybercrime's growth continued, fuelled by the COVID-19 pandemic. Responses to the pandemic, such as remote working amidst economic lockdowns and social distancing, forced governments, companies, and individuals to use the internet even more. Criminal exploitation of the pandemic through ransomware and other techniques demonstrated how little national and international law on cybercrime prevents, deters, or punishes those engaged in this activity. The pandemic spike in cybercrime underscored how criminal organizations continue to overwhelm international cooperation on cybercrime, attempts to strengthen private-sector cyber defences, and proposals to create cyber deterrence against cybercrime.

Although the pandemic postponed the negotiations scheduled for 2020, the UN process established in 2019 to develop a new cybercrime treaty has also dimmed prospects for global cooperation. This process pits authoritarian countries that support a new treaty, such as China and Russia, against democracies that oppose it, including the United States and EU members. This UN-sanctioned effort reflects years of activity by China, Russia, and supportive states to advance their interests on cybercrime and create a counterweight to the COE's Convention on Cybercrime. This fault line deepened in 2020 through more accusations from democracies that China, Russia, Iran, and North Korea provide safe havens for cybercriminals who target Western companies and who help authoritarian governments conduct cyber operations against democratic countries. A US-led summit on the ransomware threat in October 2021 among 30 likeminded countries – including Australia, Canada, Germany, India, Israel, South Africa, South Korea, and the UK – illustrated not only the worsening cybercrime threat but also the increasingly fragmented nature of international cooperation on cybercrime.

Over the past two decades, the cybersecurity issues most associated with terrorism emerged not from terrorist cyberattacks but from governments expanding electronic surveillance to counter terrorism, variously defined. Governments have not needed to use the national and international law applicable to terrorist cyberattacks, and cybercrime and cyber espionage have been more prominent threats motivating efforts to build better cyber defences. By contrast, many governments increased their surveillance powers in cyberspace to fight terrorism, which contributed to the rise of digital authoritarianism and decline of internet freedom during the 2010s.

This trend continued in 2020. Governments took advantage of the pandemic to expand their definitions of terrorism and increase their surveillance powers. The controversies that Edward Snowden triggered in 2013 about government use of cyber technologies for counterterrorism have not dissuaded many governments from engaging in pervasive surveillance and online repression in the name of defeating terrorism. The Taliban takeover of Afghanistan in 2021 following the withdrawal of US and NATO military forces caused governments to fear a resurgence of global terrorism, including more terrorist use of the internet to spread propaganda, radicalize and recruit adherents, and raise funds. This development provides governments with fresh incentives to increase their surveillance powers in cyberspace.

In 2020, democracies had to confront use of the internet by domestic extremist groups to spread propaganda, recruit adherents, and incite violence. This problem had been building for years, but the focus on the exploitation of cyberspace by foreign terrorist groups, such as Al Qaeda during the 2000s and the Islamic State during the 2010s, marginalized it. However, the ways in which domestic extremist groups used cyberspace before and during the attempted insurrection in the United States on 6 January 2021 forced democracies to grapple with the threat of home-grown terrorism. This shift in counterterrorism has many policy and legal implications, and it has re-ignited controversies in democracies about what terrorism means, whether to expand government surveil-lance powers in combating domestic terrorism, and how to respond to domestic extremists' use of encrypted communications. The struggles that democracies face with domestic terrorism created opportunities for authoritarian countries to defend, and double down on, using expan-sive cyber surveillance and repressive measures against online activities deemed to be threats to state security and social order.

7.1.2 Cybersecurity and state actors: Cyber espionage and cyber war

Cyber espionage made headlines throughout 2020. Cyber spies from various countries attempted to obtain information from US and European pharmaceutical companies about research and development on COVID-19 vaccines. The threat of Chinese cyber espionage prompted the United States and other countries to reduce or eliminate the use of Chinese technologies in national information and communication net-works. The United States acknowledged that many federal agencies and US companies were victims of the SolarWinds hack – an extensive cyber espionage operation attributed to Russia.

The SolarWinds incident highlighted poor cyber defences in the US public and private sectors and exposed the US counterintelligence com-munity's failure to detect the operation. It also demonstrated that US sanctions imposed after previous acts of Russian cyber espionage and the forward-leaning cyber posture of the US military did not deter Russia. These developments underscored, again, that domestic criminal law on espionage is not effective when international law tolerates spying, international cooperation on investigations of domestic espionage crimes is impossible, government and corporate cyber defences remain inad-equate, and governments continue to develop and use powerful cyber espionage capabilities.

In the past 20 years, much effort has gone into clarifying how international law applies to government cyber operations other than espionage in peace and war. During this time, and based on what is publicly known, state cyber operations did not cross the use-of-force, armed-attack, and armed-conflict thresholds in international law, except for possibly the Stuxnet operation. Military cyber operations conducted during armed conflict also avoided violating IHL. In 2020, there was no abatement in states engaging in cyber conflict below the use-of-force threshold and developing military cyber capabilities. These trends demonstrate that hostile cyber operations have become a pervasive type of interstate coercion and conflict short of war and will increasingly feature in how belligerents wage armed conflict in the future.

In addition, controversies with the proposed UN cybercrime treaty, the accusations that certain states collude with cybercriminals, and the escalating cyber espionage threat reflect the intensifying geopolitical competition that now characterizes international relations. Such competition makes military cyber capabilities more important, cyber coercion in peacetime more attractive, and cyber operations during war more likely. The return of balance-of-power politics does not mean that efforts to clarify how international law applies to cyber operations have failed or are doomed to failure. Rather, the changes in the international distribution of power increase incentives for states to exploit the ambiguity, uncertainty, speculation, hedging, disagreement, and controversy that persist about the application of international law. This situation is disconcerting because the window of opportunity for generating consensus among states might have closed given that, historically, *realpolitik* creates a more difficult environment for resolving differences among states about international law and non-binding norms of state behaviour.

7.2 Cybersecurity's 20 years' crisis

In his classic study of international relations, E. H. Carr described the time between 1919, after World War I ended, and 1939, when World War II began, as a 20 years' crisis. During this period, the failure of the liberal international order created after World War I produced an 'abrupt descent from the visionary hopes of the first decade to the grim despair of the second'.[1] The events experienced, and trends reinforced, in 2020 suggest that cybersecurity has suffered an equivalent crisis over a 20-year period.

When cybersecurity emerged in the first decade of the twenty-first century as a prominent policy and legal issue, the United States was the unrivalled great power, democracy and its associated human rights were ascendent, and market-based globalization made the internet and digital technologies accessible around the world. This combination of factors revolutionized communications within and across societies, produced the close association between cyberspace and democracy, facilitated multi-stakeholder internet governance, and advanced the idea of an open internet that empowered individual rights and freedoms globally. Cybersecurity problems received heightened attention, and states negotiated cybercrime treaties, began to address how terrorists used cyberspace, attempted to respond to cyber espionage, and started planning for military cyber operations in armed conflict. However, in that decade, cybersecurity challenges, and efforts to respond to them, did not threaten the preponderance of US geopolitical power, the ideological primacy of democracy, or globalization's role in disseminating the technologies underpinning the global internet.

By the end of 2020, cybersecurity – among many other policy areas – revealed that the world had changed during the second decade of the century. Chinese and Russian challenges to US global primacy succeeded in re-establishing a balance-of-power system, with the United States believed to be in decline, especially *vis-à-vis* China. This geopolitical shift contributed to the rebound and rise of authoritarianism, including digital authoritarianism, and the perception that democracies were on the defensive internationally and in disarray domestically. This ideological shift also featured authoritarian governments, led by China and Russia, increasingly subjecting domestic internet use to sovereign control, with this cyber-sovereignty strategy and its export undermining internet freedom.

Geopolitical and ideological factors converged inside authoritarian and democratic states through policies to reduce their dependence on, and vulnerability to, cyber technologies made by rival countries. China

---

[1]   E. H. Carr, *The Twenty Years' Crisis 1919–1939* (Harper Collins, 1939), 207.

accelerated its drive for technology independence, and the United States moved to reduce and eliminate the use of Chinese technologies in its networks. These efforts produced divisive competition rather than cooperative globalization in terms of existing technologies (e.g., 5G networks), emerging capabilities (e.g., artificial intelligence), and future innovations (e.g., quantum computing).

In this transformed context, cybersecurity problems reflect the geopolitical animosity, ideological antipathy, and technological rivalry now prevalent in international relations. US accusations that China, Russia, and other states conspire with cybercriminals to hurt Western companies and economies further sour an already difficult environment for cooperation on cybercrime. Even in the face of opposition from the United States and likeminded countries, China and Russia wielded sufficient clout to move UN negotiations on a new cybercrime treaty forward. China and Russia increasingly provide political and technological support to a growing number of countries interested in pursuing cyber sovereignty to fight crime, terrorism, and other security threats.

This exportation of cyber-sovereignty capabilities increases the geopolitical and ideological importance of China and Russia. It also damages internet freedom promoted by democracies. The spread of cyber sovereignty further exacerbates controversies about the definitions of terrorism and cybersecurity and underscores the lack of international agreement on the appropriate limits on electronic surveillance for law enforcement, counterterrorism, counterintelligence, and other national security purposes. Concerning crime and terrorism in cyberspace, national legal approaches are fragmenting along geopolitical and ideological lines, and the potential for states to use international law to bridge the expanding gap is diminishing.

Turning to cybersecurity threats from state actors, international cooperation on cyber espionage is now even more unlikely, especially with respect to clarifying or changing how international law applies to it. Intensifying geopolitical, ideological, and technological competition among states deepens mistrust, sows fear, and heightens national commitment to robust espionage capabilities and operations. Such competition also increases the incentives for states to develop the capabilities to engage in, and to conduct, cyber hostilities short of war for various purposes, including sabotage, retaliation, pre-emptive action, and deterrence. These incentives reduce the prospects that states could achieve, or even desire, consensus across geopolitical and ideological lines on (1) the application of international law on sovereignty, non-intervention, the use of force, and armed conflict to cyber operations; and (2) the development of non-binding norms of responsible state behaviour in cyberspace.

7.3   The next decade in cybersecurity law

The transformation of cybersecurity during the first 20 years of this century counsels caution when attempting to predict the future. Both decades demonstrate that larger, often unpredictable political forces in international relations shape cybersecurity policy and law. Even so, the changes over this period have been so significant that some speculation about what the future might hold is warranted.

7.3.1   International law

The geopolitical, ideological, and technological competition that now characterizes cybersecurity will adversely affect the role of international law in connection with crime, terrorism, and espionage in cyberspace. The synergy between digital authoritarianism and the negotiation of a new cybercrime treaty favoured by authoritarian states will fragment international law on cybercrime even more and infuse that fragmentation with geopolitical, ideological, and technological consequences. The momentum of the cyber-sovereignty approach marginalizes international human rights law relevant to conducting surveillance for counterterrorism purposes. With domestic terrorism threatening democratic governance, democracies are poorly positioned to mitigate the marginalization of human rights. Intense competition among states for power, influence, and technological advantage will prevent states from achieving meaningful agreement on increasing international law's role in regulating cyber espionage.

The dynamics for international law concerning cyber operations by states below the use of force and in armed conflict will have similar features. International legal analysis of such operations in the past 20 years has been handicapped by a limited number of publicly known operations; attribution disputes; a lack of information about operations; reluctance by states to make their practice and views on important legal issues clear; and the challenges that cyber technologies create for legal thresholds that have been controversial for a long time. The next decade will see an increase in state cyber operations and prompt more analysis of state practice under international law on sovereignty, non-intervention, the use of force, and armed conflict.

However, given heightened geopolitical, ideological, and technological competition, such analysis will have higher stakes and be more contentious. This context will not be conducive for resolving international legal questions that states have been unwilling to answer for decades, even during the more benign post-Cold War international system. During the past 20 years, states preferred legal ambiguity as they explored the potential of cyber operations. Over the next decade, this preference will deepen because states have concluded that cyber operations in peace and war have significant utility, especially in a context of intensifying interstate competition.

Fragmentation, marginalization, and contestation in international law will increase cybersecurity risks over the next decade as cyber coercion and hostilities among states escalate. For example, without feasible recourse under international law, the United States could retaliate against rival states for harbouring cybercriminals and for committing certain acts of cyber espionage to punish those states and deter such behaviour. In countering digital authoritarianism, the United States could scale-up using cyber means and methods, such as supplying dissidents with technologies to circumvent digital repression, to undermine cyber sovereignty in authoritarian states. Countries on the receiving end of such US cyber operations might retaliate, further escalating cyber hostilities in a context lacking clear legal or political guardrails on escalation. This potential for escalating cyber coercion and hostilities could spill over into non-cyber problems that are also multiplying in the international system.

7.3.2 Domestic law

The rise of digital authoritarianism and cyber sovereignty in the 2010s involved the reformation of domestic policy and legal approaches to cyberspace issues within non-democratic countries threatened by the internet freedom agenda. In the coming decade, democracies face their equivalent reckoning at the level of domestic policy and law.

First, concerning cybercrime and cyber espionage, many democratic countries, especially the United States, must use domestic law more strategically and comprehensively to build and sustain stronger cyber defences in the public and private sectors. Potential areas for the development of domestic cybersecurity law include breach notification, information sharing, risk assessment and management, insurance, standards for software development, CIP, and supply-chain assurance.

Second, the threat of domestic terrorism requires heightened policy and legal attention to how governments conduct surveillance against domestic extremists, which includes grappling with law-enforcement access to encrypted communications. In addition, and although not a cybersecurity issue, democratic governments must address the threat that online dissemination of disinformation by foreign governments and domestic actors presents, a difficult task in national legal systems that strongly protect freedom of expression and association. Third, democratic governments must continue to develop, individually and collectively, their policy and legal guardrails for cyber operations conducted below the use of force and during armed conflict because the frequency, diversity, and escalatory potential of such operations will increase.

7.4   Final thoughts

'Whoever studies contemporary international relations', Stanley Hoffmann wrote, will 'hear, behind the clash of interests and ideologies, a kind of permanent dialogue between Rousseau and Kant'.[2] Jean-Jacques Rousseau was a pessimistic realist, who saw little but competition and conflict in the intercourse among nations. By contrast, Immanuel Kant believed in the potential for perpetual peace achieved through the democratic transformation of domestic politics and the fostering of transnational economic and social relations among peoples.

In cybersecurity, this dialogue has shifted. During its Kantian phase in the first decade of this century, the belief was widespread that the com-

---

[2]   Stanley Hoffmann, 'Rousseau on War and Peace', in S. Hoffmann, *The State of War: Essays on the Theory and Practice of International Politics* (Praeger, 1965), 86.

munity of democracies could achieve and sustain global internet freedom while peacefully managing cybersecurity problems. In the second decade, Rousseau's voice in the dialogue became louder as clashing interests and ideologies among countries came to characterize international cyberspace politics. For the foreseeable future, Rousseau's pessimism will be hard to ignore in cybersecurity. Geopolitical, ideological, and technological competition now affects every domain of political action on land, at sea, in the air, in outer space, and across cyberspace. Incremental progress against cybercrime through domestic law, or more refined application of international law to state cyber operations, will not have much, if any, effect on competition, coercion, and conflict in and across these domains. Over the next decade, the nature of the permanent dialogue between Rousseau and Kant on cybersecurity will ultimately depend on what happens in international relations beyond cyberspace.

Index

Titles in the **Elgar Advanced Introductions** series include: